Shades of Loneliness

New Social Formations

Series Editor:
Charles Lemert, Wesleyan University

Shades of Loneliness: Pathologies of a Technological Society
by Richard Stivers

Ethnicity: Racism, Class, and Culture
by Steve Fenton

Public Sociology: From Social Facts to Literary Acts
by Ben Agger

Community on Land: Community, Ecology, and the Public Interest
by Janel M. Curry and Steven McGuire

Forthcoming

The Promise Keepers: Postmodern Encounters with Men on the Religious Right
by Judith Newton

Gay and Lesbian Movements in the United States: The Politics of Identity and Diversity
by Steven Epstein

"White People Are Nosey": Talking about Race
by Anne Rawls

Hours to Lose: The Shorter Work Week and the Future of Labor
by Jonathan Cutler

Global Restructuring
by Wilma Dunaway

Who Is Responsible for the Poor? Poverty and the Politics of Social Morality
by Shana Cohen

Shades of Loneliness

Pathologies of a Technological Society

Richard Stivers

ROWMAN & LITTLEFIELD PUBLISHERS, INC.
Lanham • Boulder • New York • Toronto • Oxford

ROWMAN & LITTLEFIELD PUBLISHERS, INC.

Published in the United States of America
by Rowman & Littlefield Publishers, Inc.
A wholly owned subsidary of The Rowman & Littlefield Publishing Group, Inc.
4501 Forbes Boulevard, Suite 200, Lanham, MD 20706
www.rowmanlittlefield.com

P.O. Box 317, Oxford OX2 9RU, UK

British Library Cataloguing in Publication Information Available

Library of Congress Cataloging-in-Publication Data

Stivers, Richard.
  Shades of loneliness : pathologies of a technological society /
Richard Stivers.
    p. cm. — (New social formations)
Includes bibliographical references and index.
  ISBN 0-7425-3002-7 (cloth : alk. paper) — ISBN 0-7425-3003-5 (pbk. : alk. paper)
  1. Information society. 2. Technological innovations—Social aspects.
3. Personality change. 4. Interpersonal relations. 5. Loneliness. I. Title. II. Series.
  HM851.S75 2004
  303.48'33—dc22   2003020758

Printed in the United States of America

⊗™ The paper used in this publication meets the minimum requirements of
American National Standard for Information Sciences—Permanence of Paper for
Printed Library Materials, ANSI/NISO Z39.48-1992.

To my family:
Janet, Mark, Michael, Ann, Rachelle, and of course, Moby

Contents

Foreword by Charles Lemert   ix

Acknowledgments   xiii

Introduction   1

Chapter 1   Technology, Character, and Personality   9

Chapter 2   Technology and Stress   33

Chapter 3   Cultural and Psychological Conflict   55

Chapter 4   Culture and the Neurotic Need for Affection and Power   75

Chapter 5   Compulsive and Impulsive Styles   93

Chapter 6   Narcissism and Depression   105

Chapter 7   Paranoia and Schizophrenia   125

Chapter 8   Shades of Loneliness   141

Index   145

About the Author   149

FOREWORD

~

Alone with Others

Charles Lemert

Those who have lived for any time at all on the open plains of the North American middle are drawn to each other across all that separates. We recognize our fellow citizens of the open fields and rolling hills beside the river waters. We know that they too may have been children who lay awake at night listening for the Panama Limited to whistle its way to New Orleans. We grew up listening to blues from Memphis and baseball from Chicago through the static of tiny radios smuggled under the covers. We are comforted in adult life by the chill winter sunset, red on the snowy fields awaiting spring's first cuts. We greet strangers with a familiarity bred by long days alone in hot fields or at home left by the menfolk.

One is never fully of these open fields, any more than a man of the sea belongs wholly to the vast waters. But because we have lived in them we are always from these plains settled by men and women we never knew, who braved heat and cold to defy the ever-renewing expanses that kept them from their Pacific dreams. And when one is from places like southern Illinois, or the Dakotas, or near Kansas, the places never leave our bones.

In this, as in other of his books, Richard Stivers is true to the Nebraskan he was and the Illinoisan he has become. Though he writes as a sociologist, with the accents of his profession, he resists, as plainsmen do, the fences that would keep him from grazing far and wide. Thus, he feeds the reader with startling connections and probing ideas—the kind of fodder that requires the long chew allowed by the lack of diversions for which all middle places are well-known. One thinks of others in this tradition: Erving Goffman from Alberta, Hugh Daziel Duncan (Stivers's teacher) of Southern Illinois, Alvin Gouldner of the Missouri river valley and the Illinois plains (by adoption from the Bronx), Thorstein Veblen of Wisconsin, and many more. None is quite like the others, but each stood out, as Stivers does, for a solitary way of thinking through the world.

In *Shades of Loneliness*, Stivers sets about to cover a subject that sociology, to its embarrassment, has avoided. Loneliness is, of course, a topic omnipresent in popular culture. There are self-help manuals for the lonely, biographies of leaders and writers laboring at their duties in noble solitude, and films of squint-eyed heroes tall in the saddle showing their backside to town. Yet but for a scattering of works here and there, professional sociologists have been baffled by loneliness, and thus had little to say, until now.

There is a reason for this. Sociology began, more than century ago, in the throes of a widespread anxiety as to the psychology and fate of the lonely individual. A full generation after Karl Marx painted the worker as isolated, alienated, and exploited in the factory system, the two more traditional founders of the field took up the theme. Emile Durkheim, writing at the end of the nineteenth century, was determined to establish sociology as a field independent of psychology. He succeeded at the cost of painting the individual out of his social world and diagnosing loneliness as the morbid consequence of separation from society. At the same time, Max Weber drew up the portrait of an over-organized society in which the individual was left alone, trapped in the iron cage of an overdetermined rationality. And so it happened, as time went by, that sociologists took the lead of their founding fathers and defined their mission as the work of covering any and all topics that had to do with social relations of which the limiting condition was, rather arbitrarily, the isolated individual.

Shades of Loneliness serves to put right the neglect of the fathers by picking up the themes found scattered in the traditions, but nowhere so plainly as in the famous book of a latter-day Weberian, David Riesman, whose *Lonely Crowd* is said to be one of the field's all time best-sellers. Stivers goes beyond, far beyond, this now-classic work by, first of all, observing that conformity to crowd behavior eventuates in the loss of character and in the preoccupation with personality. The personality is, in effect, the work of the solitary individual who has been pressed beyond solitude to isolation by the demands of technological society. Hence, the startlingly persuasive denouement of *Shades of Loneliness*: "One is left with the sad and shocking conclusion that schizophrenia takes the technological personality to its logical conclusion." The pathologies of technologies come to their own final expression in this paradigmatic instance of loneliness—the one cut off, not just from others but from himself; isolated by the drive to achieve a personality suitable to the world's expectations.

Shades of Loneliness requires a good long chew, but one that will be worth the while for readers daring enough to consider the terrible prospect that the world we live in induces an urge to loneliness that we, whether sociologists or common characters, would like to believe will go away of its own accord. The book gives us a bracing look at the reality hidden below the surfaces of life in the hamster cage, chasing a cure that can never end the whirl.

~

Acknowledgments

There are many to thank and undoubtedly some I have forgotten to name. The Earhart Foundation supported the writing of the book with a fellowship research grant. Diane Bjorklund, Norm Denzin, Kim Goudreau, Charles Lemert, Moody Simms, and Jim van der Laan read the manuscript and made a number of excellent suggestions. I cannot think of a group whose judgment I trust more. Bill Vanderburg and Namir Khan provided me with important references. JoAnne Geigner typed the manuscript with accuracy and a good sense of style. My friend Bob Hunt gave me the subtitle for the book; perhaps I should have asked for more.

I have been blessed with a number of outstanding graduate students the past few years., Those who have influenced my thinking include: Sally Heinzel, Steve Huchel, Mark Lindner, Brian Roessler, Grant Shoffstal, Paul Stock, Shawn Wick, Chantal Young, and Chris Young.

Charles Lemert, to whom I have been greatly indebted over the years, recommended Rowman & Littlefield Publishers to me. Dean Birkenkamp got the project started. My editor, Susan McEachern, carried it through to completion. I am grateful to her for taking over the project and offering such excellent advice. I was the beneficiary of the expertise of Chrisona Schmidt, Jessica Gribble, and Alden Perkins, as well.

My wife Janet, sons Mark and Michael, and daughter-in-law Rachelle provided me with encouragement, affection, and, unbeknown to them, ideas. Thank you all.

Introduction

Loneliness has become so pervasive in modern society that we almost take it for granted. Only something like a news item about increasing depression among teenagers appears capable of shocking us. But there are subtle indicators of loneliness, only perceptible to those who have begun to question the media assumption of universal happiness.

People seem anxious to talk to people they hardly know, going beyond politeness to the point of confession, as on television talk shows. Increasing numbers of people are willing to share intimate aspects of their life with anyone who will listen. Some even seek out crowds at the shopping mall for anonymous companionship. The inability to be alone in thought and reflection does not just characterize the young. Many of us require music, television, or radio to get anything done, and some even admit that the media are a hedge against loneliness. The fear of being alone with oneself is terrifying to those who are lonely. In this view to be alone equals loneliness.

The faces of the lonely, no longer found only among the homeless and the aged, seem fearful as well. Barry Glassner calls ours a "culture of fear" and documents how corporations, advertisers, and politicians create an exaggerated fear of things that are made to appear unusual in degree or pervasiveness, such as an epidemic of child abuse.[1] At the same time, however, there is much to fear—terrorism, global warming, nuclear war, environmental pollution, biotechnology, and growing inequality under global capitalism.

Real fears are magnified by the experience of loneliness. Real fears are intensified when people have to face them *alone* in a world without apparent purpose seemingly characterized by a relentless struggle for power.

1

In the middle-class suburbs, a kind of superficial friendliness prevails based on what M. P. Baumgartner terms "moral minimalism," avoiding conflict by not getting involved in other people's lives.[2] Not being deeply involved in someone else's life, however, rules out the possibility of passionate friendship and love and produces loneliness. This can be covered over with cocktail parties and lots of friends, even superficial ones.

Academic psychology has recognized loneliness as a widespread problem by creating a specialized area devoted to it.[3] Psychiatrist (and clinical psychologist) J. H. van den Berg maintains that loneliness is what psychiatry is about:

> Loneliness is the central core of [the patient's] illness, no matter what his illness may be. Thus, loneliness is the nucleus of psychiatry. If loneliness did not exist, we could reasonably assume that psychiatric illnesses could not occur either, with the exception of the few disturbances caused by anatomical or physiological disorders of the brain. We have no knowledge of animals ever having "genuine" mental disorders.[4]

Van den Berg's ideas suggests that all psychiatric disorders are intertwined, "a single patient, no matter to which group his illness belongs, embodies the entire psychopathology."[5] The reason for this, he argues, is that "all patients share the same human existence."[6]

But this flies in the face of the conventional wisdom of modern psychiatry that mental disorders are discrete diseases. Modern psychiatry is dominated by what Allan Horwitz calls "diagnostic psychiatry." The latter purports to leave open the question of causality, but its "medicalized system of classification emphasizes organic pathologies."[7] Modern psychiatry, moreover, promotes the idea that there are medical experts who can treat your illness with drugs, as with any other disease. Causality becomes superfluous, in this view, if the symptoms can be controlled or eliminated.

Horwitz suggests that psychiatric practitioners and the public now perceive mental illnesses as brain diseases. Earlier in the twentieth century, "dynamic psychiatry," based at least in part on psychoanalytical ideas, including that of repression, did not take this view. Yet Freud thought that someday the biological foundation of mental illnesses would be discovered. To this day many clinical psychologists and other mental health practitioners think that family dynamics are the cause of emotional problems. But in the public mind, psychiatry as a branch of medicine reigns supreme.[8]

Horwitz distinguishes between the concepts of mental disorder and mental disease. Following Jerome Wakefield, Horwitz defines a mental disorder as "a dysfunction of some internal psychological mechanism" that is socially defined as inappropriate. Internal states refer to "psychological systems of cognition, thinking, perception, motivation, emotion, memory or language." Horwitz argues that the functions these systems perform are universal to the human race. The social definition of what is inappropriate is not; it is culturally relative.[9] The concept of mental disease includes the idea of internal dysfunction but excludes the notion of socially inappropriate. Here the internal dysfunction appears to be a consequence of a physical disease. Consequently there is no need for social evaluation of how well the psychological system is functioning. Horwitz maintains that only a small percentage of mental disorders are actually mental diseases.[10]

What causes mental disorders that are not a consequence of physical disease? Horwitz rules out social factors for the most part. Following Wakefield, he suggests that natural selection is behind the individual having functional or dysfunctional psychological mechanisms.[11] I don't find this much of an explanation. When he regards the functioning of internal psychological systems as universal, Horwitz is treating them in an overly abstract way. To maintain the universality of psychological systems on the basis of their functioning is to overlook that it is not just the appropriateness or inappropriateness of the functioning of the emotional system, for example, that is culturally relative, but the context of and interrelations of the emotions as well. Emotions and emotional systems vary from culture to culture.[12] And this has serious implications for their functioning. There are psychological systems that, no matter how well they function and how appropriate they are considered, are still harmful to the members of the culture. Anthropologist Edward Sapir made this point in distinguishing between genuine and spurious cultures.[13]

The triumph of diagnostic psychiatry and its expansion into areas like social deviance represent the triumph of the medical model. More and more forms of deviance, like attention deficit disorder, are now defined as diseases. For deviance to be medicalized, Peter Conrad argues, previous forms of social control have to be perceived as failures. Then an effective form of medical control, usually a drug, has to be available, and some ambiguous organic link to the deviance must be set forth. Finally the medical profession has to be willing, usually when funding is available, to accept the behavior as a disease. Conrad maintains that the medicalization of deviance represents a technological approach to its control.[14]

William Arney and Bernard Bergen have demonstrated that the goal of modern medicine has moved from warding off death to managing life. They cite certain medical textbooks that propose "optimal life trajectories," that is, technologies of behavior from birth to death that maximize one's chances for a long, healthy, and happy life. Over against these norms of technical perfection can be charted the patient's actual lifestyle. From this utopian perspective the individual becomes a collection of deviations from the multiplicity of technical norms.[15] The task of modern medicine and related helping professions is to bring the individual's normal behavior closer to the perfect lifestyle as defined by medical technology. The theory of progress assures us that the normal and the technical will someday be one. To bring mental disorders under the rubric of mental disease plays a large part in the use of technology to control human behavior. As we will see later, technology is concomitantly a mechanism of control and the sociological factor most responsible for mental disorders. Technology is at once problem and solution.

If most mental disorders are not a result of physical disease and if natural selection is rejected as a sufficient explanation, that leaves sociological factors. The problem, as I see it, is that psychologists have for the most part ignored sociological factors beyond the family, preferring to study interaction within small groups. The tacit assumption is that culture emerges from the interaction of autonomous individuals. This is not altogether wrong, but it is misleading, since a larger culture impinges on the autonomy of the individuals who are interacting with each other.

The major psychological theories of loneliness bear this out. The social needs approach assumes that there is a universal human need for affection and friendship, which if unfulfilled results in loneliness. The cognitive discrepancy theory emphasizes the individual's expectations for companionship and intimacy; when reality falls well below expectation, loneliness ensues. The social skills orientation looks to the individual's facility for making and retaining friends—the individual's ability to make herself likable.[16] None of these theories, however, raises serious questions about how the organization of society might contribute to loneliness.

Historical and cross-cultural data indicate that a truly sociological perspective is in order. Psychologist Louis Sass argues that there is no evidence for the appearance of schizophrenia in "any significant quantity" before the late eighteenth century.[17] Van den Berg maintains that the phenomenon of multiple selves (discussed in chapter 3), a condition of the "normal" person, did not occur before the eighteenth century.[18] Clearly, both writers are contending that there is something about the organization of modern life that is conducive to psychological fragmentation.

The cross-cultural evidence is ambiguous. Sass points out that although many psychiatrists believe that the rate of schizophrenia is more or less the same (just under 1 percent) in all contemporary societies, the evidence is shaky at best. The data did not take into account the chronicity of the disorder, how quickly patients recovered, and variation in the subtypes of schizophrenia that were reported. Most importantly, he questions whether developing countries share so much with developed countries that the cross-cultural comparisons are meaningless.[19] Anthropologist Stanley Diamond maintains that there is an absence of full-blown schizophrenia in "primitive societies" because the group implicitly knows how to "set cultural limits to the process and prevent it from becoming a diagnostic entity."[20] Hunter-gatherer groups often recognize someone who is psychologically different as having unusual spiritual and healing gifts and thus channel his eccentricities into socially acceptable activities.

Victor Turner provides an example of how the community can be an integral part of healing. The Ndembu of Zambia believe that a long-standing or acute illness is caused by ancestral shades, male sorcerers, or female witches. Rituals performed to exorcise such ancestors or evil spirits tacitly assume that social conflict in the community is behind the illness. Certain persistent illnesses are believed to result from the upper incisor tooth of a hunter who dies. The tooth symbolizes the "biting" nature of gossip, jealousy, malice, and the like. On the hunter's death, relatives who are members of the Ihamba cult are supposed to carry the incisors in a pouch. If the hunter's teeth are not recovered before burial or if a relative loses a tooth, it may become embedded in someone else's body, thereby causing an illness. Everyone in the community shares the same cultural assumptions about the causes of persistent illness and the same beliefs about the efficacy of rituals to expel the ancestral shade whose tooth is embedded in the patient. Turner's doctor, a ritual specialist, performs a variety of rites and involves the community in the cure. The doctor defines his professional role as a mediator of community conflicts. The patient's disease is interpreted as evidence of dissension in the community. Public confession of the patient's conflicts with others and their antagonism toward him is used to bring the disease to a dramatic denouement. Thus the doctor's job is to restore goodwill among neighbors. Confession not only symbolically integrated the community and the spirit world but also reunited the patient with the community.[21] Turner's example, which is not unusual in the literature of cultural anthropology, suggests that traditional people possessed a wisdom about the social origins of mental disorders that we are in danger of losing.

There is reason to believe, then, that neurosis and psychosis are directly related to the social organization of modern societies. There are a few writers who have recognized this, including Karen Horney, J. H. van den Berg, Louis Sass, Joel Kovel, and David Levin, whose work is drawn on in subsequent chapters. All of them relate mental disorders to either capitalism or technology or both.

Horwitz, however, maintains that social factors rarely lead to mental disorders; rather, they can produce momentary stress that results in deviant behavior, which in turn disappears when the stress is eliminated. Someone may be momentarily depressed over the death of a relative, for example, but with time and help from friends and relatives eventually returns to normal. He admits that social factors can cause internal dysfunctions (the common characteristic of both mental disorders and mental diseases), but only under specific circumstances. A response to the stress that persists well after the stress has disappeared may be a sign of mental disorder.[22] The assumption seems to be that stress may be a "trigger" that releases an internal dysfunction of some psychological system.

Horwitz overlooks the possibility that an entire social environment may prove chronically stressful. The debilitating impact of a "spurious culture" is filtered through the actions and attitudes of families, friends, neighborhoods, and communities, which either reflect or mitigate to some extent these harmful features. The larger culture thus challenges groups and individuals; some become stronger as a result, others weaker. Over time and without decisive change, the number of those able to resist these negative pressures grows smaller. It is much like the dynamics of a concentration camp: when people are devoted *exclusively* to their own survival, it becomes increasingly difficult for others not to act likewise. I think that a technological civilization provides an extremely harmful environment. The various shades of loneliness are the price we pay for living in a society dominated by technology.

Chapter 1 discusses what I call the "technological personality," a personality that conceals an inner loneliness. Chapter 2 examines the stress (or external stimuli) that technology produces. I argue that the technological personality is reasonably well equipped to handle stress but not loneliness. Moreover, the technological personality's ability to handle stress reinforces the loneliness it experiences. Chapter 3 sets forth a general theoretical perspective for understanding psychopathology. Chapters 4–7 examine the relationship between a technological civilization and psychopathology (intense loneliness). I have organized the various disorders around the cultural contradictions of modern societies. Chapter 4 relates the conflict between the neurotic need for affection and the neurotic need for power to the cultural contradiction between love and power. Chapter 5 examines obsessive-compulsive and impulsive-neurotic styles in relation to the contradiction of rationality and irrationality in a technological civilization. Chapter 6 relates narcissism and depression to the contradiction between power and meaning; chapter 7 considers paranoia and schizophrenia in relation to the contradiction between unity and fragmentation. In chapter 8, I demonstrate how the disorders and the cultural contradictions are interrelated. I am not suggesting that these disorders exhaust the list of psychopathologies; only that they are important and illustrate especially well the connections between mental disorders and a technological civilization.

My approach to the subject matter of this book—loneliness—is naive, that is, unspecialized. My experience as a mental health practitioner is limited, and I am a sociologist. This would seem to disqualify me from writing a book that begs for psychiatric and psychological expertise. Van den Berg has indirectly offered a response to this objection. He maintains that all who suffer from different disorders share a common human existence and also suggests this about the normal and the pathological.[23] All of us share this human existence. And no one is an expert on it. Sometimes specialized knowledge (knowledge of the part) can get in the way of understanding the whole.[24] My goal is to provide the broadest perspective on loneliness in a technological civilization.

Will mental health practitioners find this book useful? Although it does not provide them with a new diagnostic tool kit or a new treatment, it does help them understand how the context of the patient's complaints about himself and his associates and his mode of psychological adaptation have been provided by the larger society. The therapist can then understand that, in van den Berg's terms, a neurosis is simultaneously a "sociosis" (a disorder of society).[25]

Notes

1. Barry Glassner, *The Culture of Fear* (New York: Basic, 1999); see Frank Furedi, *The Culture of Fear* (London: Cassell, 1999), for a different interpretation.

2. M. P. Baumgartner, *The Moral Order of a Suburb* (New York: Oxford University Press, 1988).

3. Ken Rotenberg and Shelley Hymel, eds., *Loneliness in Childhood and Adolescence* (New York: Cambridge University Press, 1999).

4. J. H. van den Berg, *A Different Existence* (Pittsburgh: Duquesne University Press, 1972), 105–6.

5. Van den Berg, *Different Existence*, 3.

6. Van den Berg, *Different Existence*, 4.

7. Allan Horwitz, *Creating Mental Illness* (Chicago: University of Chicago Press, 2002), 3.

8. Horwitz, *Creating Mental Illness*, 1–5.

9. Horwitz, *Creating Mental Illness*, 26.

10. Horwitz, *Creating Mental Illness*, 13.

11. Horwitz, *Creating Mental Illness*, 11.

12. Catherine Lutz, *Unnatural Emotions* (Chicago: University of Chicago Press, 1988).

13. Edward Sapir, "Culture, Genuine and Spurious," in *Culture, Language, and Personality*, ed. David Mandelbaum (Berkeley: University of California Press, 1970), 78–119.

14. Peter Conrad, "On the Medicalization of Deviance and Social Control," in *Critical Psychiatry*, ed. David Ingleby (New York: Pantheon, 1980), 102–19.

15. William Arney and Bernard Bergen, *Medicine and the Management of Living* (Chicago: University of Chicago Press, 1984), chaps. 7, 10.

16. Daniel Perlman and Monica Landolt, "Examination of Loneliness in Children-Adolescents and in Adults: Two Solitudes or Unified Enterprise," in *Loneliness in Childhood and Adolescence*, 339.

17. Louis Sass, *Madness and Modernism* (Cambridge: Harvard University Press, 1992), 364–65.

18. J. H. van den Berg, *Divided Existence and Complex Society* (Pittsburgh: Duquesne University Press, 1974).

19. Sass, *Madness and Modernism*, 361–64.

20. Stanley Diamond, "Schizophrenia and Civilization," in *In Search of the Primitive* (New Brunswick, N.J.: Transaction, 1974), 354.

21. Victor Turner, "An Ndembu Doctor in Practice," in *Magic, Faith, and Healing*, ed. Ari Kiev (New York: Free Press, 1960), 230–63.

22. Horwitz, *Creating Mental Illness*, 29–37.

23. Van den Berg, *A Different Existence*, 4.

24. See Richard Stivers, *Technology as Magic* (New York: Continuum, 1999), chap. 5, for a discussion of how many forms of therapy that purport to be specialized scientific techniques actually function as magical practices.

25. J. H. van den Berg, *The Changing Nature of Man*, trans. H. T. Croes (New York: Norton, 1961), chap. 3.

~

CHAPTER ONE

Technology, Character, and Personality

Character and Personality

Character and personality are complex terms. In everyday discourse character appears to refer largely to the moral dimensions of the self, to the practice of virtue. Some academics also use the term in this sense.[1] I will use the term in different ways, depending on the level of analysis—individual or cultural—and the historical period.

Following David Riesman, I regard social character as a mode of conformity.[2] The broad cultural definition of the self establishes the form and the limits in which personality develops. Whereas each personality, or total self, is unique, social character, cutting across social divisions, is more or less universal in a society. Social character is the cultural form of personality.

Before examining Riesman's character types, I will draw a distinction between the aesthetical and the ethical, and there is no better source than Søren Kierkegaard for these important concepts. The aesthetical and the ethical are both dimensions of culture and "existence-spheres," that is, ways of orienting oneself to the world and ways of acting. Social character is the cultural definition of an existence-sphere.

The aesthetical has to do with how things impact our senses. Are they agreeable or disagreeable, pleasurable or painful, beautiful or ugly, interesting or boring? Such experiences can then be represented in art, literature, music, and dance, which in turn create an aesthetic response in us. The ethical is concerned with requirements and limits in our relationship to others. It seeks to define what is good and, by contrast, what is bad, and hold us accountable

9

to the good. If art (in a general sense) is concerned with the aesthetical, morality centers its attention on the ethical.

The aesthetical and the ethical are distinct aspects of culture, but they interact with each other. Art sometimes takes moral issues as a theme, just as morality can become aestheticized so that the pursuit of pleasure (consumption today) becomes a requirement.

At the level of individual existence, or existence-sphere, the aesthetical is concerned with immediate experience.[3] Aesthetic existence is principally about enjoyment: to live for the moment, to lose oneself in the pleasure of the moment is the aesthete's goal. Yet possibility, the possibility of even greater pleasure, is more important than reality.[4] The wish to transform reality, to make it yield still more pleasure, is the ultimate ideal of an aesthetic existence. A purely aesthetical approach to life, Kierkegaard observes, is ethically indifferent to others. When one is not ethically bound to others, one is free to relate to them as if in a game, attempting to gain the advantage.[5]

The ethical sphere of existence is concerned with the requirement that places the individual in a struggle with the immediate—instinct and emotion. When one is ethically victorious, one overcomes selfishness. With the movement to the ethical existence-sphere, one assumes responsibility to others and to oneself. For Kierkegaard there is no freedom without responsibility and moral authority because humans are naturally selfish. Freedom involves conflict, not the least of which is the conflict with excessive authority. Too little and too much authority diminish the possibility of freedom.

The ethical sphere of existence provides a moral unity to the self; one is the same person, no matter what the circumstances. When one stands for certain beliefs and puts them into action, one thereby becomes a consistent, unified self. To paraphrase Kierkegaard, one chooses a self for a lifetime. The aesthetical approach to life cannot provide unity for the self because there is no unity in pleasure.[6] Instead, there is self-abandonment as one merges with the object of pleasure. Therefore, an aesthetical approach to life entails a multiplicity of selves—a different self in each situation.

Possession of a moral self makes one not only consistent but also coherent, both to self and others.[7] Others can understand me and I can understand myself only when I possess a consistent, unified self. The result is a certain transparency in my actions, a unity of motive and action.

No one, however, lives entirely in one existence-sphere. At the very least an aesthetically oriented person tends to turn aesthetical pursuits into moral absolutes. Friedrich Nietzsche is the most obvious example. For Kierkegaard, personality is the integration of extant aesthetical qualities into the moral self: immediate enjoyment becomes subordinate to ethical considerations.[8] A personality, a unitary self, is first and foremost ethical in nature.[9] This is obviously at odds with our current aesthetical understanding of personality.

Western ideas about the total self or personality have changed dramatically since the sixteenth century. Lionel Trilling argues that the aesthetical concept of authenticity superseded the ethical concept of sincerity in the nineteenth and twentieth centuries.[10] Drawing on the work of writers, critics, and philosophers, he has fashioned a complex story that is as revealing about the larger culture as it is about the self. I will briefly summarize his argument.

The term *sincerity* arose in the sixteenth century coeval with the decline of feudalism and the secularization of society, and especially as the cultural emphasis shifted to the individual. Sincerity as it applied to humans (objects at one time could be called "sincere") originally referred to an individual who consistently practiced virtue. But no sooner was it applied to human relationships than it was applied to society as a whole. Hence a sincere society was one in which the actual conduct of the citizens more or less corresponded to the stated morality and one in which society actually encouraged the sincerity of its citizens. By the eighteenth century, however, there was a growing recognition that societies might hinder the consistent practice of virtue. To know whether or to what extent a society hindered or assisted the sincerity of its citizens required critical judgment about society. The individuality of the citizen was thus reinforced. Sincerity provides for an intensified awareness of one's personal identity, which potentially comes from opposition to society as much as identification with it.

The term *sentiment of being,* so popular in the eighteenth century, referred to the individual's self-consciousness or awareness of his own existence. The "honest soul," or sincere person, was in the best position to possess this sentiment of being. Although Rousseau is often identified with modern individualism, his view of the self is essentially moral.[11] He decidedly rejects the aesthetical self and the corresponding emphasis on art as a model for existence. Rousseau has two major objections to art: it is a force for conformity and it leads to a repudiation of the self. In the former instance, art either helps form public opinion or creates subcultures of its own. The latter criticism pertains to the issue of role-playing with its model of the theater. Along these lines, Denis Diderot's *Rameau's Nephew* explores the implications of feigning over against being.[12] Rousseau may have fathered modernity, but it became a disobedient child.

The nineteenth century was the scene of the great reversal: the aesthetical dimension of culture became more important than the ethical dimension. Sentiment of being was redefined. Being true to virtue is less important than being true to one's emotions. Sentiment of being refers to the strength of the passion, to the energy that is felt and expressed. Initially the term *sublime* was more important than the term *beauty* in the new artistic lexicon, for the former contained the idea of *strength* of experience. Eventually the concept of sentiment of being was incorporated into the idea of personal authenticity. To be authentic is to follow one's own desires, feelings, and creative spark— to be *autonomous*. No one exemplifies this autonomy more than the artist. The work of art was now regarded as autonomous, and the artist even more. During the Romantic period the artist, the creator, becomes more important than the work of art, which is not bound to the principle of mimesis.[13]

The criticism of society encourages the rise of authenticity as a seminal idea of the nineteenth century. The civilizing process, as Norbert Elias calls it, depends on the moral constraint of one's feelings and desires. Society could be so repressive, it was argued, that it becomes inauthentic. Under these circumstances one would need to invert society's values. The opposition of self to society was radical. The developing logic of authenticity turned morality into a purely societal phenomenon and left the emotions, instinct, and creativity solely to the individual. Writers like Oscar Wilde and Friedrich Nietzsche were so hostile to the idea of sincerity and the unified moral self that they praised role-playing and wearing masks in everyday life. Personal autonomy had become banal.

The inversion of ethics and aesthetics was now complete. Trilling characterizes the reversal as the "experience of art projected into the actuality and totality of life as the ideal form of moral life."[14] Martha Wolfenstein referred to one popular version of this in the mid-twentieth century as "fun morality."[15]

The emphasis on authenticity, the aesthetic sphere of existence, took hold more quickly in Europe than in North America. This was due in part to an aesthetic lifestyle being the province of artists, intellectuals, and members of the aristocracy, which by the eighteenth century had been stripped of many of its former duties and functions. The United States possessed no aristocracy and its writers and artists had less influence on society than their counterparts in Europe. In America, as Tocqueville noted, middle-class virtues were in the ascendancy.

If the British viewed themselves through the concept of sincerity into the nineteenth century, Americans perceived themselves in terms of the concept of character.[16] Character was an essentially moral concept that stressed the virtues associated with the "Protestant ethic"—fortitude, industry, thrift, sobriety, prudence—and more traditional virtues such as courage and honesty. American public schools and universities regarded the character building of its students as one of their most important purposes.[17] Organizations like the Boy Scouts and the YMCA, which originated in England, reinforced the character building of church (Sunday school) and school.[18]

It was not until the early twentieth century in America that the term *personality* began to supplant *character*; it was a largely aesthetic conception of the self. The self that was redefined in terms of self-expression, self-fulfillment, and performance was a personality. The advice manuals of the period gave less moral instruction than recommendations about style.[19] Manners, for instance, were not so much about virtuous action as about the impact of action on others: pleasure and influence.

To summarize, the term *character* is an ethical conception of the self, just as personality is an aesthetical conception. The historical change from character to personality parallels that from sincerity to authenticity. In both these distinctions, the emphasis is on the total self. Social character, as I am using the term, refers to the cultural mode of conformity and limits the development of the self. Hence we should find that changes in the cultural definition of the self perfectly reflect changes in the dominant mode of conformity.

In *The Lonely Crowd*, Riesman identifies three types of social character that have existed throughout history: tradition-directed, inner-directed, and other-directed. The latter two types are the ones that will most concern us. Riesman relates the three types to demographic and other historical changes, and here his theory is weakest. But his discussion of the three character types is rich and suggestive.[20]

The tradition-directed type is prevalent in hunter-gatherer or precapitalistic agricultural societies. Traditions in the form of rituals and mythical beliefs take precedence over individual rationality. For our purposes the critical issue is that there is no full sense of individuality present so that members of society are similar in most important respects. This character type is moral in that the sacred traditions that form the basis for conformity are ethical in nature. The chief psychological control in this type of society is shame. You only know you have done something wrong if others shame you through ridicule, censure, or ostracism.

The inner-directed character type, according to Riesman, arose in the Renaissance and Reformation. Individuality, at least its secular versions, reached its fullness then and continues into the present.[21] This social character type has two major aspects: the internalization of moral values (a conscience) and clearly articulated goals, often economic. The inner-directed person is "driven" to achieve his goals, but his conscience limits both the goals and the means by which they are achieved. The inner-directed individual internalizes goals and normative attitudes that family, teachers, and religious leaders have established for him. Under the best of circumstances, when those in authority want the young to be independent—both free and responsible—the individual acquires a measure of control over the goals and attitudes he internalizes.

The inner-directed type possesses a distinctively moral orientation, which, combined with its individuality, produces a certain protection against peer pressures. The paramount form of psychological control is guilt; the inner-directed type experiences guilt even when no one is around to shame him. The self-unity of the inner-directed type is provided by its inner direction, or conscience. This sometimes makes the inner-directed person appear rigid, especially to someone who is other-directed.

The other-directed character type is a recent development, beginning perhaps in the nineteenth century and coming to fruition in the mid-twentieth century.[22] Unlike the previous two character types, the other-directed type is aesthetical in orientation; it is primarily concerned, at the beginning of the twenty-first century, with consumption. The dominant mode of conformity is adjustment to the peer group, which in Riesman's felicitous phrase is a "tutor in consumption."[23] The peer group's norms and those of the media (which become increasingly important) consist of transitory norms of taste, what's in, what's cool, what's fun.[24] Because those aesthetic norms are ephemeral, they are not internalized.

The most important product today, Riesman argues, is a personality.[25] Like all other products it must be highly differentiated, if only in superficial ways. Consumption extends to everything from politics to personality: we become connoisseurs and consumers of the personalities of others.[26] Within the peer group, however, lies pervasive competition. Riesman refers to peer group members as "antagonistic cooperators," who are competing for popularity, friendship, and at times leadership. Psychological control is based on diffuse anxiety: one is never sure where one stands with others.

It is important to account for the authority of the peer group and especially public opinion over the individual. Why has public opinion supplanted family, school, and religion as a source of authority? I closely follow Kierkegaard on this point. The latter sources of authority are moral, and they entail a passionate relationship between those with authority and their subordinates. But our age, Kierkegaard says, is one in which a common morality has weakened if not dissipated; moreover, public opinion has supplanted it.

The public is formed not only by the mass communication media but also by individuals becoming detached observers of others.[27] The condition of being an onlooker to life involves a complex of intellectual and psychological processes: reflection, envy, and moral *ressentiment* (destructive envy that desires less to imitate the other than to see him brought down to one's level). Kierkegaard opposes reflection first to passion, then to action.

In a period of moral dissolution, relationships between individuals become ambiguous as the aesthetical interests of each party are in conflict and yet remain partially concealed. It is not always polite to admit one's selfish motives. This leaves the individual in a state of "reflective tension." Rather than an inward relationship regulated and given meaning by moral qualities such as trust and love, the relationship has become external. In Kierkegaard's formulation, passion can only be expressed by those whose relationship to others is inward—ethically qualitative. With the decline of inwardness and passion, one's relationship to the other becomes concurrently that of aesthetic possibility and ethical indifference. As such the relationship must necessarily become abstract, the object of theoretical reasoning (reflection). Life in a "reflective age" assumes the characteristics of a game in which one plots one's moves in advance in order to maximize one's chances for pleasure or success.

Reflection itself, Kierkegaard maintains, is not the problem, but rather reflection that does not result in action—reflection that becomes an escape from action. When reflection is not accompanied by inward moral commitment, envy ensues. The powers of reflection are at the disposal of selfish desires. One envies others their possessions and their accomplishments. At this point Kierkegaard draws a startling conclusion about the modern reflective and passionless age: "envy is the negative unifying principle."[28] The envy within the individual has its counterpart in the envious attitudes of others, and this collective envy is chiefly expressed through public opinion.

When the envy that is present in reflection as aesthetic possibility is not accompanied by decision and action, it spills over into moral *ressentiment*. *Ressentiment* is present in every age, but what makes it different in the modern era is "leveling." By this Kierkegaard means the attitude that no one is better than anyone else. Because of a lack of moral character, the individual denigrates and even ridicules those who have distinguished themselves. It is not enough to admire and envy the other: one must tear him down. To be effective, leveling must be done in concert with others; it is essentially a collective phenomenon. Whereas it was once the province of a social class or occupation, in a reflective and passionless age it is accomplished by the public. The public is an abstraction in that the members do not interact with one another; therefore, the public's opinion must be expressed through the mass media. Because moral *ressentiment* takes the form of leveling in a time of passionless reflection, and because leveling is expressed through public opinion, public opinion both creates and is an expression of the "negative unity of the negative reciprocity of all individuals."[29] We can thus understand the tendency of the media, even more so today, "to level" every politician, movie star, and celebrity. The individual has become a "fractional part" of the public and as such delights in leveling. Public opinion, in Kierkegaard's formulation, expresses desire (positive up to the point of selfish envy) and *ressentiment*. Our pseudo-intimacy and pseudo-cheerfulness conceal envy and fear that can only safely be expressed in public opinion.

The peer group too is a fractional part of the public; its unity is based in part on its ability to level and scapegoat outsiders. The hostility of the peer group, however, can readily be turned on anyone who fails to conform to its views. One's status within the peer group is invariably uncertain. This accounts for the fear of isolation and "diffuse anxiety" Riesman discovered in the other-directed peer group. Even more than capitalistic competition, leveling is responsible for this anxiety. Indeed, envious reflection and *ressentiment* in the form of leveling are behind the emergence of the other-directed character type. The aesthetical approach to life leaves one under the sway of public opinion and peer group pressure.

The other-directed character type is a cultural form in which individual personalities (total self) develop. The aesthetical term *personality* replaced the ethical term *character*, just as the other-directed social character type supplanted the inner-directed type. The aesthetical term *personality* reflected in some ways what individual personalities were experiencing. Moreover, as we will see later, scientific psychology arose in part to study highly differentiated personalities and to determine normal development. Public opinion and psychology unintentionally joined to help regulate the variegated manifestations of an aesthetical lifestyle.

Technology, Experience, and Meaning

In chapter 3, I will articulate a theory of the technological society. For now I wish to examine certain cultural and psychological consequences of modern technology. Technology is the paramount determining factor in modern societies. Technology here refers to both material technology (machines and tools) and nonmaterial technology (organizational and psychological technique). Bureaucracy is an example of organizational technique; advertising, of psychological technique. Both material and nonmaterial technology are oriented to efficiency; hence they can be considered one phenomenon. Technology organizes not only our relationship to nature but also our relationships to one another; moreover, it has transformed all forms of social organization. Yet technology is concurrently a major disorganizing force in society, for in its modern form it results in cultural disintegration (suppression of meaning) and personal alienation (suppression of subject).[30]

The suppression of subject refers to individual actions, individual experience, and interpersonal experiences. Technology makes human relationships abstract and thus impersonal. The objectified nature of technique denies the subjectivity of both user and recipient. As a rational, objective method, technique turns the object of technique into an abstraction. For instance, suppose that as a parent I read the book *Parental Effectiveness Training* and decide to rear my children according to this technique. Rather than adjust my method of child rearing to the individuality of each child and to the total context of family relationships, I am now going to use a unitary method, which, if applied religiously, will purportedly made each child manageable and thus a standardized product.

The same denial of subjectivity and individuality happens to the user of the technique. Even if substantial effort is required to learn a technique, once it is learned, the user is relieved of personal responsibility in judgment and choice. In our previous example of the technique of child rearing, the parent using *Parental Effectiveness Training* gives up learning about his children and exercising moral judgment and becomes an appendage to the technique. Note that the subjectivity and individuality of each party in a relationship is threatened by the presence of the technique. The subjectivity of the parent is denied in part by not taking into account the subjectivity of the child.

The proliferation of techniques for relating to others is unrelenting. The largest section of many bookstores is the self-help section (relationships, self-improvement, addiction/recovery). Technique is being applied to every human relationship, even sex and religion.

Sexual technique reaches beyond sex toys, sex clinics, videotapes, and sex manuals: tabloids, women's magazines, and even the usually staid *Reader's Digest* have articles on sexual technique. The smashing of the old sexual taboos has merely substituted one form of guilt for another. Now people feel guilty not because they have sex outside of or before marriage, but because they do not have it or do not have it often enough, or have not achieved enough orgasms for themselves or their partners. Our culture has made romantic love dependent on sexual fulfillment and turned sex into an objectified activity—a logical process with steps, the modern sport.[31]

The same holds true for religion. For over a century, religion promoted itself as a psychological technique, a technique for achieving peace of mind, health, happiness, and sometimes success.[32] By the middle of the twentieth century this had become the dominant characteristic of what Will Herberg called the actual American religion—the "American Way of Life."[33] Management techniques are taught in seminaries, as are counseling techniques. Churches often employ marketing strategies to reach new or hard-to-reach members. Finally, churches sometimes use the mass media to dramatize their message, raise money, and attract potential members.

If technique now mediates virtually all human relationships, then social institutions have lost their efficacy. Social institutions comprise a collective set of experiences that are embedded in traditions and moral norms. Just as technology diminishes personal experience, it conspires against interpersonal or collective experiences. Arnold Gehlen observed that technological societies were supplanting institutions with organizations. Given that most organizations are bureaucratic (organizational technique), this means the further extension of technology.[34]

The transfer of function from institution to organization assumes the form of the technical expert. Authority, which was traditionally centered in parents, teachers, religious leaders, and politicians, was institutional in nature (e.g., familial, religious, political). This cultural and personal authority has given way to the power of the expert. Typically experts work for organizations.

Take the family as an institution, for instance. Alexis de Tocqueville observed in the nineteenth century that the authority of the father was being supplanted by government and public opinion.[35] Today myriad governmental agencies regulate how parents rear their children, requiring medical tests and treatment, education, discipline, and so forth. Perhaps more important is the gallimaufry of helping professionals or mental health experts, whether housed in school, clinic, or doctor's office, that advises parents about the "normality" of their children. Eventually vocational counselors and teachers assist the child in choosing a career. Parents' main purpose, seemingly, is to provide their children emotional sustenance and recreational activities. But even here there are enormous difficulties. Children's recreation, at least in middle-class families, is so highly organized that parents are reduced to chauffeurs and spectators. Coaches and recreational experts instruct the children; parents reinforce the directives of the experts and thus become their subordinates.

Even with respect to affection, children partially withdraw from parents at ever earlier ages to find their home in the peer group. M. P. Baumgartner's study of a suburb demonstrates that children live most of their life outside the home. She characterizes domestic relations as "loose-knit," resulting in "weak families." Family members spend much of their limited time together in passive entertainment, and parents go to great lengths to avoid conflict. In such a context, there are weak social ties and minimal obligations of mutual aid. Baumgartner refers to this arrangement as "moral minimalism."[36] One psychiatrist compared the modern family home to a motel.[37] What family relationships remain are largely aesthetical and consequently ambiguous.

The most critical objectification of experience occurs in the mass media for a number of reasons. First, the media are the paramount source of information for most people. Second, reality appears to be in the media. There appears to be a one-to-one relationship between visual images and reality, even though the media necessarily take images out of their cultural and historical context and thus reconstruct them.[38] But the media also deal in possibility—especially technological possibility. Hence everything important and everything possible are on television and the Internet.

In the media, language has become subordinate to visual images so that the latter is experienced as the "meaning" of the former.[39] This is a materialization of language. The primary impact of visual images is emotional. Indeed, the media provide us with a series of vicarious experiences that make our own lives pale by comparison.

The media are likewise experienced as an authority. In reflecting on his own child's inability to distinguish television from reality, Jerry Mander remarks that *"Seeing things on television as false and unreal is learned."*[40] Edmund Carpenter reports on an informal study of college students who were told that television reporting on an event was inaccurate. The students either accepted the inconsistency uncritically or doubted reality. Television is an emotional authority.[41]

The media objectify experience because they deny imagination and the application of symbols to one's own experiences. This can be readily illustrated. When I read a novel, I imagine the characters and events through a series of mental images[42] that are not as precise, and certainly not as materialistic, as visual images. Each reader has a different set of images about the novel. But the movie about the same novel objectifies the experiences so that the audience has identical images.

The Technological Personality

The objectification of experience has had a profound influence on the modern personality. Personality is now characterized by two dialectics: the objective and the subjective and the inner and the outer. This is in sharp contrast to pre-eighteenth-century personality, for which the distinction between objective and subjective and inner and outer was much less pronounced.

The objectification of the personality is aided by the loss of judgment and responsibility. Human technique obviates the need for judgment, decisions, and responsibility. Consequently the individual is extremely vulnerable to those objectivizing tendencies. Technology colonizes our experiences, opinions, emotions, and consciousness. I have already noted how technology objectifies experience, both individual and collective.

Just as technology leaves us with secondhand experiences, it provides us with secondhand opinions. Public opinion is based on secondhand knowledge rather than experience or readily intelligible facts. Public opinion is a necessary component of a mass society; it is a substitute for interpersonal knowledge that arises from practical, everyday life in the context of intense familial and community relations. The mass media provide us with ersatz experiences on which opinion rests. If personal knowledge is phenomenal, public opinion is epiphenomenal;[43] it is concerned with what most of us know little about through experience or serious thought. Therefore public opinion is secondary both in regard to its source—the mass media—and its type of knowledge— epiphenomenal. More obvious than the artificial character of public opinion is its fragmentation.[44] There is no coherence or continuity to the totality of opinions. A sure sign of fragmentation is the inconsistent (if not contradictory) quality of many opinions. For example, American opinion supports preserving the environment and economic growth simultaneously. Opinions are always out of context, for issues are presented to the public consecutively as self-contained entities; they resemble facts that appear to be autonomous. The fragmentation of opinion reflects the fragmentation of information conveyed through the media.[45]

Partly as a consequence of fragmentation, public opinion is based on simplified issues.[46] Complex and profound problems can only be resolved, and even then rarely, through long and arduous discussion. Because opinion forms (or is pressured to form) on an enormous number of issues, many of which are outside most people's personal expertise, the media must simplify the issue. Only then can public opinion emerge. Criticism of American politicians, for example, sometimes centers on their tendency to simplify issues, when the problem is actually much more a result of the mass media, which can only operate profitably through simplification, and the public, which, no matter how well educated, due to technical specialization, is ignorant about most issues.

If public opinion is knowledge (albeit simplified and secondary) at one level, it is desire (and fear) at another. Public opinion is ultimately about what one desires to occur or wishes to be eliminated or controlled. This is evident in the very terms under which opinion is solicited—"agree or disagree," "yes or no," "approve or disapprove," "like or dislike." Public opinion tends to follow the desire that technology's promise unleashes and advertising presents to us. Therefore public opinion is decidedly ephemeral.[47] Its "norms" change as everyday life changes and new objects of desire emerge.

Secondhand opinion is a hybrid—part superficial knowledge and part desire. Secondhand experience and secondhand opinion result in a loss of a sense of reality. Heavy television viewers experience the greatest distortion of reality.[48] The loss of a common symbolic reality, which only language can provide, necessarily results in the loss of a sense of reality. Those who are dominated by visual images have a false sense that reality is on television and in the computer, the two sources of most of our information.[49]

Secondhand emotions originate in the media. The media, which provide us with vicarious experiences, are dominated by visual images whose fundamental appeal is emotional. Consequently, in viewing television programs, movies, and computer videos, we experience emotions that are shallow and transient. Moreover, they become what Arnold Gehlen has called "emotional schemata," or emotional stereotypes.[50] Emotionally we are like Pavlov's dogs, responding to emotional conditioning.

When a subjectivity based on lived experience is emptied out and replaced with objective images, the personal and impersonal are inverted. In recent years people have grown more willing to reveal intimate details of their personal lives to casual acquaintances or even strangers. The model for this, of course, is the talk show; ordinary people along with celebrities proclaim that they once were drug addicts, experienced child abuse, or suffered from illiteracy. When we share intimate details of our lives with acquaintances and strangers, our discourse resembles the *anonymous* discourse of the mass media. It is no longer important to whom we address our remarks.

Even as we divest ourselves of our personal lives, we attempt to become personal by identifying with celebrities and even products on television. There are a couple of reasons for this. One is that reality is in the media, and the celebrities have lives infinitely more interesting than our own humdrum lives. Another is that we know more people in the media than in real life, and we know them more intimately.[51] Most of our relationships except for family and close friendships are superficial. Indeed, research indicates that we feel closer to television personalities than we do to acquaintances, and the strength of this feeling is a close second to what we feel for our friends.[52]

We come alive and become interesting by living through and resembling these celebrities and other advertised products. We are thus objectified as images. What prevents everyone from becoming the same image object is the myriad ways of "assembling" one's total image. This totality is always changing because the images we live in and through can readily be substituted for others. Life as represented on television and the other media is an experimental life.

Consciousness usually contains personal experience and emotion, but technical consciousness does not. It reduces every activity and relationship to an instrumental one and turns knowledge into abstract information.

Technical rationality makes up an ever increasing part of individual consciousness. We become full-time consumers of technical information both at work and at leisure. The excessive information available on the computer and in the media, Ellul notes, turns us into "exclusive consumers," with the result that even shopping for and acquiring consumer goods becomes a means of gathering and using information.[53] That is, we become connoisseurs of technical products. Even if one only owns an inexpensive and simple music system, one can become a connoisseur by gathering sophisticated information about speakers.

Technical rationality is collective and impersonal; it does not depend on experience, practical knowledge, or moral judgment. Moreover, the growth of technical rationality implies a fractionalized consciousness. This involves not only the split between collective rationality and subjective reason but also the fragmentation within technical rationality itself because of specialization.[54] Technical information is unintegrated culturally and therefore proliferates wildly and appears to be random. Information is never neutral; it directs our behavior, including moral conduct. The most important information in traditional societies was practical knowledge useful for group survival that was given symbolic meaning. Information about hunting, for example, described traditional ways of hunting and explained how the deities or their representative, the "master of the hunt," provided the animals, which humans had to respect even as they hunted. Practical knowledge thus was ritualized because it was set in a narrative about the meaning of hunting.

Today information tends to go in opposite but mutually reinforcing directions. Knowledge has become abstract, both as theoretical knowledge and technical knowledge.[55] Technical knowledge tends to supplant tradition or common experience in providing information that is practical in the sense of efficient, objective (decontextualized), and meaningless. Such abstract information is not sufficient to meet human emotional needs. Traditional information did this by providing a symbolic context for practical knowledge. As shared meaning declines in a technological civilization, knowledge must develop that is emotional as an end in itself rather than as an epiphenomenon of shared meaning. Emotional knowledge becomes a compensation for abstract knowledge, especially technical knowledge. And the most prevalent sources of emotional information today are the televised and computerized visual image.

How does the individual respond to the reification of experience, knowledge (opinion), emotion, and consciousness? In traditional societies much of what today is considered objective knowledge (technical knowledge) was a kind of symbolic intersubjective knowledge. This practical knowledge was embedded in a cultural matrix that narrowed the gap between subjective and intersubjective experience. Objectivity becomes a problem when it is cut loose from symbolic meaning, for then it appears to be inorganic. The individual intuitively feels menaced, indeed overwhelmed, by a nonliving objectivity. As Owen Barfield has observed, throughout most of history humans identified objectivity with organic nature, a living whole that was experienced as having an inward consciousness. By symbolizing nature, humans "participated" in creating and maintaining it.[56] Objectivity was experienced as intersubjectivity. Because technology at a certain threshold weakens, if not destroys, symbolic meaning, today the objective and subjective are at odds. That is, human subjectivity is a reaction against the objectification of human experience, knowledge, and emotion, but a reaction that does not permit escape.

Technical consciousness is an abstract, impersonal consciousness. This "cold" consciousness, Erich Kahler argues, has contradictory consequences: greater insensibility and greater sensibility.[57] The former refers to depersonalization or detachment. Insensibility to another's plight or even my own means that I analytically search for the causes of the misfortune and what remedies there are for it, instead of responding intuitively, emotionally, and with moral judgment. In so doing we "deaden" ourselves against suffering and become indifferent to others even though we may urge political action or contribute to charity.

At the same time, however, technical consciousness produces a greater sensibility to visual stimuli. Alfred Crosby has demonstrated that prior to the late Middle Ages Western civilization relied more on touch and hearing than sight.[58] But beginning in the thirteenth century an emphasis on synthesizing visualization and quantification led to the technological mastery of life. Today we live in a world in which visual images are dominant and are proliferating rapidly. We have become connoisseurs of visual details, not those necessary for survival as with a hunter-gatherer group but those consumed for the aesthetic pleasure of the detail. We also become more sensitive to the personalities of others and acquire a hyperreflexivity about ourselves. Ulrich in *The Man without Qualities* perfectly illustrates the new insensibility and sensibility.

The new sensibility reinforces the tendency to differentiate one's personality from that of others. Georg Simmel observed in 1900 the tendency to emphasize accidental details such as hairstyle as important aspects of personality.[59] The reason he gives is the standardization effected by the "social-technological mechanism." The money economy, bureaucracy, and the political state create rules that make citizens increasingly similar. To struggle against this standardization, the individual emphasizes the aesthetic details of the self that have come to constitute personality.

The loss of direct experience results in a loss of a sense of reality. In a technological civilization, a shared symbolic reality gives way to a reified reality—in the media and on the computer. Reality is always somewhere else. The individual compensates by creating her own imaginary world. An apt example is a factory worker who performs boring, repetitive tasks while living in a world of daydream and fantasy. A meaningless existence demands an imaginary world. The loss of a feeling of reality likewise unleashes desire, which is the mechanism of fantasy. Advertising preys on this vulnerability by creating a fantasy world of desirable products. Moreover, this world of desire and fantasy overflows the boundaries of the self into human relationships. We end up expressing absurd and extravagant opinions on matters we know little about.[60] With technology so dominant, subjectivity is narrowed to human instinct.[61] At least my instincts, such as aggression and sexuality, belong to me.

At the inner core of this new subjectivity is loneliness and fear of others. Behind these feelings are a sense of meaninglessness and a sense of powerlessness. Technology appeals to our will to power. It provides us with a false sense of power: technology's (the automobile, the computer) power is my power. In contradictory fashion, however, it contributes to a "confused sense of impotence." Because that power is really not my power. Humans cannot keep up with the speed, power, and information processing ability of machines, computers, and technological systems. Moreover, the increase in information about technological means and technological objects may lead to a failure to make a choice. Too many choices and too much information about them can create a situation of sensory and intellectual overload with a resultant feeling of impotence. The pervasive but tacit sense of powerlessness today is a reaction to the overwhelming and universal power of technology.

Feelings of powerlessness and meaninglessness are mutually reinforcing. There is an inverse relationship not only between power and moral values (a type of symbolic meaning) but also between technical information and symbolic meaning. The excess of information in a technological age results in a "broken vision of the world." One loses a sense of the past, the ability to evaluate the present in terms of the past. The triumph of the computer and the visual images of the media produce a "culture of forgetting."[62] Studies indicate that our memories decline to the extent that everything is done for us (the computer) and shown to us (the images of the media). Memory centers on events that have acquired emotional, intellectual, or moral significance to us. The past understood in either mythological or historical terms acquired meaning through key events that took on symbolic meaning. The information from the computer, as already noted, is abstract, logical, and quantitative, but ultimately meaningless. The cynical worldview of the computer is that we live in a random and meaningless world about which the omnipotent computer can generate an infinite amount of information that we can exploit to our advantage.

Symbolic meaning, by contrast, provided humans with a measure of power. Historically, symbolization was a way for humans to gain control over their milieu. By enveloping it within their symbolic system, even as they were acknowledging its greater power, they gained a sense of mastery. Ellul argues that the human ability to symbolize has been the single most important factor in the cultural evolution of the human race.[63] Because technology is our own creation, we do not perceive a need to symbolize it in the traditional sense. It is only when we confront a foreign power—nature—that we bring it within our symbolic net. Symbolization simultaneously creates a meaningful world and allows us to *distance* ourselves from this world. Without effective symbolization, we have no way to keep technology from invading and conquering culture.

The rise of technology and the decline of a common morality involve the erosion of moral meaning and a tacit feeling of powerlessness. Feelings of meaninglessness and powerlessness extend beyond technology to human relationships. With the loss of a shared morality and the proliferation of techniques to control others, we are "freer" to manipulate and exploit others. Of course, they are just as free to do the same to us. The destruction of a common morality means that we are not morally obligated to help others; nor can we expect assistance from them. Without a minimal level of trust that a common morality provides, human relationships become vague and dangerous.[64] When human relationships become uncertain, competitive, and potentially hostile, the individual protects herself by failing to express her true feelings to someone who, in all likelihood, is concealing his motives as well. Human relationships become an arena in which individuals play a number of roles, feign certain emotions, and manipulate others to their advantage. To be alone, however, is not necessarily to be lonely. Loneliness arises in a context of meaninglessness and powerlessness, and it brings with it a fear of others.[65]

There is a way to describe modern subjectivity: puerilism. If modern technology tends to diminish normative reason, responsibility, personal experience, and moral judgment, then it renders us childlike. J. H. Huizinga has provided important insights about modern puerilism. The paramount characteristic of puerilism is the inversion of work (and every serious activity) and play. We treat play (e.g., sports, television programs, video games, and entertainment in general) with a seriousness that borders on fanaticism. Witness the growing fervor of sports spectators all over the world and the amount of television coverage given sports. Concomitantly, we regard the serious activities of life, such as business and politics, as a game whose sole purpose is to gain personal advantage over others. The global economy has institutionalized business as a game.

Huizinga observes that the sentimental idealization of youth, so prevalent in the mass media, is the work of adults. The so-called youth culture is the expression of a technological utopianism that extols the health and happiness of the human body.[66] Both in terms of physical development and freedom from responsibility, youth symbolizes these cultural values. Examples of puerilism include "the need for banal entertainment" and the "search for gross sensations," which are characteristic of a state of "permanent adolescence."[67] This is akin to Robert Pattison's definition of the vulgar in the context of rock music: "common, noisy, crass, and untranscendent." The vulgarian simply follows his instincts.[68]

Communication too has become vulgar. The widespread use of slogans, intolerance toward the opinions of others, excessive flattery, and the expression of unbridled instincts are all signs of puerilism.[69] Mass entertainment is for the most part easily recognizable as puerile. Comedy has become gross, cruel, and stupid. Beavis and Butthead and Tom Greene are examples that readily come to mind. Sports participants and their fans seem to compete to see which group can be more juvenile. Trash talking, finger pointing, the wave, chanting, loud booing, the intimidation of referees, and fights on the field and in the stands are not the actions of adults.

The modern personality is puerile in its subjectivity, but the inner core of this subjectivity implies that the child is lonely and fearful. Just as the decline of a common symbolic intersubjectivity created a tension between the objective and the subjective (the latter a compensation for the former), so too did it effect a contradiction between the inner and outer dimensions of personality. The outer surface of the technological personality, seemingly, is the opposite of the lonely child but compensates and covers for it.

The outer surface of the personality is flexible, adjusted, outgoing (friendly and garrulous), confident, and mildly hyperactive. This is the personality that modern organizations[70] require and the one that is represented in the media in the form of the celebrity. Flexibility means that one can and will play any role one is given. Good role players engage in deep acting. Surface acting, according to Arlie Hochschild, entails feigning certain feelings toward someone with full consciousness that one feels otherwise;[71] deep acting involves a more complete assimilation of the role to the self (at least for the duration of the scene) through repeated commands to the self (a kind of self-hypnosis) or by imaginatively constructing the desired emotions internally. Deep acting is more tiring because it temporarily requires a greater transformation of the self, but it is more convincing.

Adjustment suggests that one is a "team player," one who "fits in." The adjusted person makes a home in the group or organization and more than anything else fears rejection. Flexibility and adjustment together create the "obedience to authority" mind-set that enables one to simply follow.

In his classic *The Organization Man*, William Whyte suggested that managers are expected to be outgoing even in private life in the suburbs.[72] The outgoing, friendly, talkative, and confident individual has a better chance of manipulating customers, employees, and neighbors than the introverted person has. Because we are all expected to be like this, we demand this of each other; we don't like diffident and reserved people.

With the decline of a common morality, every relationship becomes one of power: *adjust* to greater power and *manipulate* lesser power.[73] The technological personality contains both dimensions. It stretches from one pole to the opposite so that any individual's personality falls somewhere in between in terms of emphasis. Some of us are more adjustment oriented, whereas others are more manipulation oriented. Flexibility allows one to fit in, whereas being outgoing, friendly, confident, and talkative facilitates the manipulation of others. The model for the technological personality is in the media—the celebrity.

No one has understood the celebrity's relationship to television better than George Trow. The celebrity is the personification of television. The "cold child" is Trow's name for television. On television, his home, the celebrity has a short attention span and is self-indulgent, like a child. Moreover, he exudes pseudo-cheerfulness and pseudo-intimacy, but it is a cold or false cheerfulness and intimacy. The pseudo-cheerfulness and pseudo-intimacy are anonymously directed to anyone watching, the potential consumer. They are cold, manipulative emotions. The celebrity links television with its audience by providing vicarious experiences and feelings of love. This love, however, turns out to be nothing more than familiarity. The celebrity is of course associated with products so that the latter come to embody the qualities of the former. As Trow notes, "The most successful celebrities are products. Consider the role in American life of Coca-Cola. Is any man as well loved as the soft drink is?"[74] No wonder we wear our clothes as advertisements.

What is the relationship between the inner core of the modern personality—the lonely and fearful child—and the outer core—the outgoing and confident child? The head of the outgoing, confident child rests on the body of the lonely, fearful child. The former is a comment on and compensation for the latter. J. H. van den Berg has observed that modern people talk for the sake of talking. It is of no interest to them what the talk is about.[75] Who better fits this description than the celebrity? Trow suggests that television is about pseudo-intimacy and that only celebrities have dual lives—an intimate life and a lonely everyday life in a mass society.[76] Only celebrities appear fully human. Getting to know them seems to bring an end to a mild but endemic loneliness.

This consideration of the two dialectics of the technological personality— from the objective to the subjective and from the inner to the outer—suggests that there is little genuine individuality left to the modern self. The technological personality is a creation of modern organizations and the mass media. The technological personality is the self that a technological civilization demands and creates; it is the objectification of the other-directed character type.

Notes

1. See, for example, James Davison Hunter, *The Death of Character* (New York: Basic, 2000); and Lester Hunt, *Character and Culture* (Lanham, Md.: Rowman & Littlefield, 1997).

2. David Riesman, *The Lonely Crowd* (New Haven: Yale University Press, 1969), chap. 1.

3. Søren Kierkegaard, *Stages on Life's Way*, trans. Walter Lowrie (New York: Schocken, 1967), 430.

4. Søren Kierkegaard, *Concluding Unscientific Postscript*, trans. David Swenson (Princeton: Princeton University Press, 1941), 288.

5. Søren Kierkegaard, *The Present Age*, trans. Alexander Dru (New York: Harper & Row, 1962).

6. Søren Kierkegaard, "An Occasional Discourse," in *Upbuilding Discourses in Various Spirits*, trans. Howard Hong and Edna Hong (Princeton: Princeton University Press, 1993), 7ff.

7. Jacques Ellul, *The Betrayal of the West*, trans. Matthew O'Connell (New York: Seabury, 1978), 44–49.

8. Søren Kierkegaard, *Either/Or*, pt. 2, trans. Howard Hong and Edna Hong (Princeton: Princeton University Press, 1987), 177ff.; see also Harvie Ferguson, *Melancholy and the Critique of Modernity* (London: Routledge, 1995), 98–99.

9. In *Stages on Life's Way*, Kierkegaard discusses a third existence-sphere—the religious. The ethical sphere of existence can only be understood as a transition to the religious sphere. In *Concluding Unscientific Postscript*, he even identifies two "boundary zones," between the aesthetic and the ethical, as well as between the ethical and the religious.

10. Lionel Trilling, *Sincerity and Authenticity* (Cambridge: Harvard University Press, 1972).

11. Tzvetan Todorov, *Frail Happiness*, trans. John Scott and Robert Zaretsky (University Park: Penn State University Press, 2001).

12. Trilling, *Sincerity and Authenticity*, 7–75.

13. Tzvetan Todorov, *Theories of the Symbol*, trans. Catherine Porter (Ithaca: Cornell University Press, 1982), chap. 6.

14. Lionel Trilling, *The Opposing Self* (New York: Viking, 1955), XIV.

15. Martha Wolfenstein, "The Emergence of Fun Morality," *Journal of Social Issues* 7 (1951): 15–25.

16. Hunter, *Death of Character*, 7; see also Warren Sussman, "'Personality' and the Making of Twentieth-Century Culture," in *New Directions in American History*, ed. John Higham and Paul Conkin (Baltimore: Johns Hopkins University Press, 1979), 212–26.

17. Hunter, *Death of Character*, chaps. 2–3.

18. Hunter, *Death of Character*, 57–59.

19. Hunter, *Death of Character*, 7.

20. Riesman, *Lonely Crowd*, chap. 1.

21. Mircea Eliade, *The Myth of the Eternal Return*, trans. Willard Trask (Princeton: Princeton University Press, 1954), 102–12, argues that Judaism provides the earliest implicit concept of individuality in the sense that God loves each individual person equally.

22. Riesman notes that Tocqueville points out the American's dependence on public opinion but argues that the nineteenth-century middle-class individual is "decisively different" from his twentieth-century counterpart. In other words, Riesman does not find continuity between the nineteenth and the twentieth centuries. When Kierkegaard's views on nineteenth-century public opinion are brought into the discussion, it will become apparent that a strong case can be made for continuity between the nineteenth and the twentieth centuries. Admittedly, there has been an intensification of this tendency.

23. Riesman, *Lonely Crowd*, 80.

24. The relationship between peer group attitudes and public opinion is symbiotic. Peer group attitudes and desires are expressed through public opinion, which in turn influences peer group taste. The link between the two is the mass media. Public opinion can only be expressed through the mass media, which has a direct impact on the individuals who compose the peer group. The peer group simultaneously helps create public opinion and carries it. Because of the enormous power of the media, however, the peer group, whose main purpose is consumption, is a passive agent of change. That is, its desires and demands are set in the context of technological possibility; consumers may get what they demand, but only after the media have created a need by symbolizing consumer goods so that they become embedded with qualities, lifestyles, and power.

25. Riesman, *Lonely Crowd*, 46.

26. Riesman, *Lonely Crowd*, 81.

27. Kierkegaard, *Present Age*, 64.

28. Kierkegaard, *Present Age*, 47.

29. Kierkegaard, *Present Age*, 52.

30. Jacques Ellul, *Perspectives on Our Age*, trans. Joachim Neugroschel, ed. Willem Vanderburg (New York: Seabury, 1981), 49–50.

31. Richard Stivers, *Evil in Modern Myth and Ritual* (Athens: University of Georgia Press, 1982), 21–25.

32. Donald Meyer, *The Positive Thinkers* (New York: Pantheon, 1980).

33. Will Herberg, *Protestant, Catholic, Jew* (Chicago: University of Chicago Press, 1983), chap. 5.

34. Arnold Gehlen, *Man in the Age of Technology*, trans. Patricia Lipscomb (New York: Columbia University Press, 1980), 163.

35. Alexis de Tocqueville, *Democracy in America*, Vol. I, trans. George Lawrence (Garden City: Anchor, 1969), 584–89.

36. M. P. Baumgartner, *The Moral Order of a Suburb* (New York: Oxford University Press, 1988), chap. 3.

37. Herbert Hendin, *The Age of Sensation* (New York: Norton, 1976).

38. Jacques Ellul, *The Humiliation of the Word*, trans. Joyce Hanks (Grand Rapids, Mich.: Eerdmans, 1985).

39. Richard Stivers, *The Culture of Cynicism* (Cambridge: Blackwell, 1994), 151.

40. Jerry Mander, *Four Arguments for the Elimination of Television* (New York: Quill, 1978), 252.

41. Edmund Carpenter, *Oh, What a Blow That Phantom Gave Me!* (New York: Holt, Rinehart & Winston, 1973), 61–66.

42. Paul Ricoeur, "Imagination in Discourse and in Action," *Analecta Husserliana*, ed. Anna-Teresa Tymieniecka (1978), 3:3–22.

43. Daniel Boorstin, *Democracy and Its Discontents* (New York: Random House, 1974), 20.

44. Boorstin, *Democracy*, 19.

45. Neil Postman, "The News," in *Conscientious Objections* (New York: Knopf, 1988), 72–81; see also Mark Crispen Miller, *Boxed In: the Culture of TV* (Evanston: Northwestern University Press, 1988), 3–27.

46. Jacques Ellul, *Propaganda*, trans. Konrad Kellen (New York: Knopf, 1969), 205–6.

47. Jacques Ellul, *The Political Illusion*, trans. Konrad Kellen (New York: Knopf, 1967), 49–67.

48. George Gerbner and Larry Gross, "Living with Television: The Violence Profile," *Journal of Communication*, Spring 1976, 192.

49. Richard Stivers, *Technology as Magic* (New York: Continuum, 1999), 68–78.

50. Gehlen, *Man in the Age of Technology*, 78–79.

51. Jay Martin, *Who Am I This Time?* (New York: Norton, 1988), 219–20; John Caughey, *Imaginary Social Worlds* (Lincoln: University of Nebraska Press, 1984), chap. 2.

52. Charles Leroux, "Our Electronic Friends," *Chicago Tribune*, May 6, 2001, sec. 2, pp. 1, 6.

53. Jacques Ellul, *The Technological Bluff*, trans. Geoffrey Bromiley (Grand Rapids, Mich.: Eerdmans, 1990), 330.

54. Erich Kahler, *The Tower and the Abyss* (New York: Braziller, 1957), chap. 1.

55. Ellul, *Technological Bluff*, 327–28.

56. Owen Barfield, *Saving the Appearances* (New York: Harcourt, Brace & Jovanovich, 1957), 96–116.

57. Kahler, *Tower and the Abyss*, 91–97.

58. Alfred Crosby, *The Measure of Reality* (New York: Cambridge University Press, 1997).

59. Georg Simmel, "The Metropolis and Mental Life," in *The Sociology of Georg Simmel*, trans. Kurt Wolff (New York: Free Press, 1950), 409–24.

60. Gehlen, *Man in the Age of Technology*, 55–56, 121–22.

61. Stivers, *Culture of Cynicism*, 151–52.

62. Ellul, *Technological Bluff*, 330.

63. Jacques Ellul, "Symbolic Function, Technology, and Society," *Journal of Social and Biological Structures* 1 (1978): 207–18.

64. J. H. van den Berg, *The Changing Nature of Man*, trans. H. F. Croes (New York: Norton, 1961).

65. Both Kierkegaard and Tocqueville observed in the nineteenth century that people had begun to experience a mild fear of others on a daily basis.

66. Stivers, *Culture of Cynicism*, chap. 3.

67. J. H. Huizinga, *In the Shadow of Tomorrow* (New York: Norton, 1936), 170–82.

68. Robert Pattison, *The Triumph of Vulgarity* (New York: Oxford University Press, 1987), 6–7.

69. Huizinga, *In the Shadow of Tomorrow*, 170–82.

70. See Robert Jackall, *Moral Mazes* (New York: Oxford University Press, 1988), for an enlightening discussion of the personality demanded by modern corporations.

71. Arlie Hochschild, *The Managed Heart* (Berkeley: University of California Press, 1983), 33–42.

72. William Whyte, *The Organization Man* (Garden City, N.J.: Anchor, 1956), 388.

73. Stivers, *Culture of Cynicism*, chap. 4.

74. George Trow, *Within the Context of No Context* (New York: Atlantic Monthly Press, 1981), 48.

75. J. H. van den Berg, "What Is Psychotherapy?" *Humanitas*, Winter 1971, 358.

76. Trow, *Within the Context*, 48, 73.

CHAPTER TWO

~

Technology and Stress

Modern technology not only helps create a personality type but also generates a great amount of stress. Stress is a universal phenomenon, but its forms and the human response to it are culturally and historically specific. The main issue in this chapter is how the technological personality confronts various kinds of stress and eventually internalizes them.

"Stress" is a general term that refers to almost any negative aspect of life. In this discussion I will use it to refer to aspects of our physical and social environments that threaten our comfort or well-being and "demand" a response. We will consider kinds of stress that are based in the physical and social environments; interpersonal conflict, which can also be considered a source of stress, will be discussed in subsequent chapters.

Categories of Stress

There is a growing body of research and theory on environmental stress.[1] It is not my purpose to clarify and resolve the different interpretations of stress. Some approaches emphasize its physiological aspect; others focus on its psychological dimension.

Some think of stress in the context of brain activity, others in the context of the ability to process information, and still others in the context of systems theory (the relation of the demands of the environment to the individual's ability to control the environment).[2] Despite the variety of perspectives on stress, there are some common insights and categories in its study.

The earliest sustained studies of stress were about physiological responses to physiological challenges in the context of disease. The "pathogen model" of stress helped call attention to the consequences of long-term exposure to stress: exhaustion and a lower resistance to disease. In this view, the problem is not merely stress but its persistence.[3]

Increasing attention has been devoted to psychological stress as a factor that accompanies physiological stress or as a factor in itself.[4] In the case of potential environmental stress, the individual's interpretation of the situation is its psychological mediation. Is the event (source of the stress) perceived to be threatening, harmful, or just challenging? Moreover, what is the meaning of the potentially stressful event? For example, one man's music is another man's noise. Experience plays a major role in psychological stress. Personal knowledge about the detrimental effects of long-term exposure to loud noise may increase the level of psychological stress one experiences in such a situation, for instance. Furthermore, some sources of stress in the environment possess symbolic meaning. Loud music of certain types may come to symbolize unruly teenagers, who are themselves perceived to be a source of stress. The perception of whether one can control the source of stress also has some impact on how stress is experienced.[5]

The experience of stress leads to "coping" behavior. How does one respond to the stress? There appear to be two principal ways. One is manipulation; for example, the individual either removes the stress or leaves the scene of the stress. The other is adjustment; for example, the individual attempts to change her internal environment. Drugs, alcohol, meditation, and relaxation exercises may distract one from the stress.[6]

Psychological stress may continue well after the source of the stress has been attenuated. Moreover, chronic or repeated stress may produce an effect that is a consequence of continuously responding to stress—an aftereffect. There are both physiological and psychological aftereffects. Psychological aftereffects may include "decreases in cognitive functioning and reduced tolerance for frustration, aggressiveness, helplessness, decreased sensitivity to others, and withdrawal."[7] In this chapter, we will examine the main sources of environmental (physical and social) stress and how the technological personality reacts to it.

The Tempo of Society as Stress

"Tempo" is a musical term that designates the rate of speed at which a composition is played.[8] It sometimes refers to the speed at which life is led. The term "pace of life" is often substituted for "tempo of life," but Robert Levine maintains that the former term encompasses more than the latter. Pace of life includes speed as well as the "tangled arrangement of cadences" and "perpetually changing rhythms and sequences, stresses and calms, cycles and spikes."[9] Pace of life encompasses social time in its entirety. Since most people experience social time in terms of tempo,[10] I will use the term "tempo" interchangeably with "pace of life."

Like other animals, humans have bodily functions and processes that are timed to nature, the circadian day, and seasonal cycles.[11] Industrialization altered the natural rhythm of human existence, first at work and later at leisure, as people were forced to keep pace with the machine. Today the computer imposes its time—the nanosecond—on people. Obviously the tempo of life is accelerating.

Research on the personal experience of tempo has identified several categories, first, time urgency. This may include a preoccupation with time, rushed speech, rushed eating, driving too fast and impatiently, constantly making lists and schedules, impatience when waiting, and feeling irritable or bored with nothing to do.[12] Time urgency entails a compulsion to do as many things as rapidly as possible. We seem to suffer from a sense of "time scarcity."[13] Other aspects of tempo include the perceived speed of the workplace and the speed outside the workplace, for example, family, leisure, and the preferred level of activity in life as a whole.[14] Modern technological societies operate at a high tempo. Technology has shrunk time and space, thereby permitting us to live and work ever more quickly. Not all of this speed is experienced as stress, however, as we will see below.

The tempo of television commercials, television programs, and films has accelerated.[15] Commercials contain the most hyperactivated imagery. There are an average of ten to fifteen image changes per thirty-second commercial and seven to ten per sixty-second segment during a typical television program.[16] The tempo of films has likewise increased. Many today complain about slow-moving films that feature dialogue and character development. The faster and more frenzied the action the better. Events and time become accelerated, condensed, and thus simplified. Consequently the media are the great equalizers. Between television and the computer, amusement is conducted at an ever accelerating pace. Because the media produce ersatz norms,[17] especially for heavy users, there is a sense that to avoid boredom, life outside the media should be fast paced.

Consumption, which is enforced and must keep up with production, is also accelerating. Economist Steffan Linder identifies three forms that the acceleration of consumption assumes. The first is "simultaneous consumption," when an individual uses more than one consumer product simultaneously, for example, reading, watching television (even several programs), listening to music, and carrying on a conversation. The second form is "successive consumption," which refers to using products or services consecutively but decreasing the time spent on each activity. For example, instead of playing eighteen holes of golf, one plays nine holes and then immediately goes fishing for several hours. The third form involves substituting a more expensive version of a consumer product for a less expensive version in response to advertising intended to turn us into connoisseurs, first at the level of information and then at the level of experience.[18] The three forms are interrelated and derive from the cultural belief that the meaning of life resides in consumption.[19]

Perhaps there is no better example of the acceleration of consumption than tourism.[20] Travel in the nineteenth century was leisurely and often undertaken for economic, political, and cultural reasons. By the second half of the twentieth century, tourism, which has little in common with travel, had become a major industry. Tourism mastered "successive consumption" by packaging as many tourist sites and countries into the shortest amount of time possible; moreover, tourist enterprises provided consumers with simultaneous activities on the tour bus or ship, for instance, food, music, lectures, movies, and so forth. The goal is to persuade the consumer to "upgrade" his tour next time with an even better product.

The acceleration of family life received less attention than that of work until fairly recently. Arlie Hochschild's insightful study of how families manage "time urgency" is especially helpful because she looks at work and family concurrently. She argues that work has become more humanized, whereas the home has become more industrialized. More and more parents try to become efficiency experts at home to meet the demands of marriage and family life. Of course both parents working exacerbates the situation. The number of organized activities outside the home that children participate in has been increasing. Hochschild terms this "domestic outsourcing": recreation, counseling, tutoring, music lessons, sports, and meals often occur away from the home. Consequently, dutiful parents act as travel agents and cab drivers for their children.[21]

The consciousness of time scarcity in the family is expressed in the term "quality time." Although parents spend only limited time with their children, it can be so intense and meaningful that the quality of their time together more than compensates for its brevity. One problem is that quality time lends itself to superficial amusement instead of serious discussion, which takes more time than "quality time" permits. Hence quality time becomes a reward that guilty parents bestow on their children.[22]

The hectic pace of life that children experience reaches its culmination in college. David Brooks writes about students at Princeton University who are so busy that they have to make appointments to see their friends.[23] The proliferation of external organized activities in childhood is an apt preparation for college.

Related to the tempo of life is the experience of simultaneity, which entails the compression of quantitative time and the loss of qualitative time. It is a long-standing cliché that our lives are ruled by the clock. Following Benjamin Franklin we know that "time is money" and that punctuality is a virtue. Moreover, we suffer from time scarcity in modern societies because we "spend" so much time at work, shopping, servicing our possessions, and pursuing leisure.[24] The latter (leisure) maintains the hectic pace of the former (work).

The computer creates a synchronous society by reducing time to ever smaller units. The computer produces the experience of the instantaneous as it processes increasingly enormous amounts of information in nanoseconds. As Jacques Ellul observes, "Real time, in which the computer now functions, is a time looped in advance and made instantaneous." With the assistance of the computer, technology "programs time," that is, it subordinates time to its own functioning rather than to human existence.[25] As such it reduces the past and future to the present. But because the present is shrinking to the nanosecond, technology appears to exist outside of time.

In addition to reducing quantitative time almost to the zero point, technology destroys qualitative time. Technology makes tradition, memory of the past, and experience irrelevant, for it objectifies experience. The past ceases to be a living past and exists merely as history. A living past is organized around symbolic events that serve as key elements of a group's identity.

Likewise technology makes the future as the meaning of history superfluous. A qualitative future requires that history be open, not predetermined in the process by which the future is realized. But technology attempts to control the future by eliminating it, that is, by creating the eternal present of a technological utopia.[26] The myth of progress promises a future that, despite its accidental differences, is only a repetition of the present.[27]

What are the consequences of a faster tempo of life that borders on an experience of simultaneity? First, there is a decline in memory. The more we are forced to live almost exclusively in the present, the more the past fades from memory. We only remember what is important to us, and increasingly what is important is reduced to our private existence. Second, the quality of decisions suffers.[28] Reflection cannot be hurried; it requires time to integrate information, see relationships, and make judgments. As Ellul has noted repeatedly, a technological civilization demands reflex, not reflection. Decisions tend to be automatic in furthering the cause of technological growth. Critical reason, which requires time and solitude, becomes scarce in a technological civilization. Third, there appears to be a decline of pleasure.[29] To be distinctly pleasurable, an event needs to be experienced in a relaxed, not a hurried, fashion. Our harried existence reduces the opportunity for intense pleasure. Quantity replaces quality.

If pleasure (or at least conscious pleasure) is declining, ecstasy is on the upswing. Ecstasy is an altered state of consciousness. Mysticism is a form of ecstatic experience, as is the "high" that results from frenzied activity (e.g., long, intense exercise or loud, repetitive music). Ellul argues that much ecstasy today is "a function of the acceleration of the tempo of the technical society."[30] Echoing this, Milan Kundera mentions that "speed is the form of ecstasy the technical revolution has bestowed on man."[31] Perhaps he should have said that speed is the main cause of ecstasy today, for to act by reflex for long periods results in a state of ecstasy.

Tempo alone is not responsible for the widespread experience of ecstasy; it is also a consequence of the regimentation of existence. As bureaucratic and technical rules proliferate, humans sense that they have lost personal control over their lives. Escaping into the realm of ecstasy seems to be rebellion against a too rational, too orderly existence.[32] Drugs, alcohol, sex, violence, music, and video games are all forms of ecstatic escape. Technology directly produces ecstasy through the tempo it imposes on society and indirectly produces it as compensation for regimentation. Some of the compensations for the impact of technology (e.g., computer games) mimic and thus reinforce the tempo of a technological civilization.

Communication as Stress

Part of the reason for a harried existence is the incredible proliferation of information and visual images. A technological society has a voracious appetite for technological information; technology exists as a system because of the information that permits the coordination of technologies separated in space. The very devices, however, that allow us to communicate technical information also provide a vehicle for the communication of superficial information, rumors, and gossip. Never before have so many said so little about nearly everything. Cell phones, e-mail, fax machines, the Internet, conference calls, and telepresence provide a technological environment of continuous communication. Moreover, the visual images of the mass media provide a distraction from the rigors and abstractness of a technological environment. We produce and consume an enormous amount of information.

Jacques Ellul argues that an excess of information has a number of negative consequences.[33] First, too much information becomes disinformation. We are unable to integrate the specialized and sometimes trivial bits of information that threaten to overwhelm us because distinguishing between relevant and irrelevant information is increasingly difficult. Without a common culture that filters and integrates knowledge, individuals have to decide for themselves what is relevant.

Second, this inability to integrate information results in a "broken vision of the world." We concentrate on information about the present with little memory of the past. Because the past has meaning only as part of a cultural memory (an essential component of being able to face the future with confidence and hope), the past without meaning is only history to be enjoyed, if at all, as an aesthetic experience. It is not morally compelling in the way tradition is; hence, it is easily forgotten. As a consequence we become prisoners of the moment.

Third, an excess of information results in our becoming "exclusive consumers." We consume information more than goods: to be rational consumers, we must first collect information about the product or service. Advertising, moreover, attempts to turn us into connoisseurs of products. Even if we cannot actually afford to participate as connoisseurs, we can read about sports cars, sound systems, and the like. Because this information is provided for us, we depend less on ourselves to make judgments and decisions and fend for ourselves. Consumers become slaves to expert information.

Excessive information therefore produces a "confused sense of impotence." Not only is my personal knowledge inadequate, but I am sometimes unsure about the sources of my knowledge. Not all expert opinion is expert; some is mere opinion. Worse yet, much of it has been created not to expand our knowledge but to sell a product or advance a cause.[34] Dependency on expert information combined with doubts about its veracity produces a tendency to postpone (if not fail to make) important choices others have made for us. This is undoubtedly behind the high percentage of eligible Americans who fail to vote.[35]

The most important source of information for most people is still television.[36] But it supplies decontextualized information that lacks the temporal and spatial contexts of everyday life; its reality is anytime, anyplace. Space in the sense of place is meaningful to humans insofar as it is part of a cultural heritage. The places where key events occurred acquire a symbolic meaning, becoming metaphors for a group's identity and hooks on which to hang memories of the past. Traditional societies often perform rituals at the real or imagined place where such events have occurred. Rites of renewal, for example, honor the time and place of the creation of the world or the birth of a society.

In creating an "eternal present," television eliminates the historical context of events. It places us exclusively in the present—a random, incoherent present.[37] Existence has been typically experienced as a narrative myth, or history in the case of a society and biography in the case of an individual. Narrative contains two main characteristics: temporal succession and transformation.[38] Temporal succession can either be continuous—duration time—or discontinuous—event time. Although narrative includes duration time, its paramount concern is event time. Television in its overall impact is antinarrative. It flattens out event time, thus turning event time into duration time.

The visual spectacle of television conjures up a feeling of apocalypse, the end of the world. In studies of the effect of television violence on viewer attitudes, George Gerbner and Larry Gross demonstrate that heavy watchers (four or more hours a day) perceive the world to be a violent, scary place and exaggerate their own risks, in part because the "world of television drama is, above all, a violent one in which more than half of all characters are involved in some violence."[39] Beyond the violence, television produces, on a purely emotional level, a sense of catastrophe, of the end.[40] Every natural disaster, every war and political uprising, every despoilment of the environment, every personal tragedy in the world, is compressed into a thirty-minute news program. In traditional societies people confronted local tragedies but not global ones. Emotionally, then, viewers experience the world of television as a place of ever escalating disasters.

Television exacerbates the sense of disaster and doom in two related ways. First, along with technology in general, it destroys the need for memory.[41] Visual images become a substitute for memory. Television requires us to live in an unstable present in which memory only gets in the way of the pleasurable loss of self that comes from vicariously living through images. The decline of memory leaves us more anxious about life's problems because we do not have the benefit of learning how others have reacted to similar problems.

Second, on the level of visual images, television imprisons us in a frightening reality. Without the attribution of meaning, reality becomes even more terrible, even more unbearable than it would be otherwise. Television and visual spectacle in general empty existence of meaning. This contributes to the sense of apocalyptic doom, for hope derives from a sense that ultimate meaning will someday transform reality.

Television, however, makes the apocalypse pleasurable. Television is the key factor in turning life into a series of spectacular images to be consumed and enjoyed. At the very least the encounter with the end of the world on television is interesting. In the novel *Mao II*, one of Don DeLillo's characters, a photographer, doubts the validity of her attempt to shock people about the squalor of the world: "And no matter what I shot, how much horror, reality, misery, ruined bodies, bloody faces, it was all so fucking pretty in the end."[42]

We are bombarded daily with a barrage of information and visual images; moreover, we are communicating with one another at work and at home with ever greater frequency. The Internet allows us to chat with people we don't know. Seemingly this should produce a greater feeling of closeness to others, a greater sense of community. But the opposite seems to occur.

In a much cited article, psychologists Robert Kraut and Vicki Lundmark studied the effects of Internet use on ninety-six families over two years. They were specifically interested in its impact on social relationships and psychological well-being. The more time individuals spent online, the greater the degree of depression and loneliness they experienced. This is perfectly understandable because increased Internet usage resulted in some loss of close friendships.[43] Face-to-face friendships sustain us emotionally. Relationships that are not based on shared responsibilities, shared difficulties, and shared experience, like online relationships, are superficial and unsatisfactory. Obviously the quality of communication is much more important than the quantity.

Crowding and Noise as Stress

Those who study environmental stress distinguish between natural habitat and "built habitat" as environments. I want to focus on stress in the built habitat, especially crowding and noise. Crowding or high density, which has been well studied, is correlated with high blood pressure, frequency of illness, anxiety, discomfort, aggressiveness, and learning disabilities.[44] Most people dislike crowding except for short periods under special circumstances (e.g., being part of a crowd at a football game).

The severity of the stress depends on the human response to it. One's prior experience with crowding may mitigate some of the psychological discomfort because one knows how to act in a crowd to protect one's autonomy. A fan who attends a crowded football game may learn how to handle obnoxious fans, how to avoid long lines, and how to maximize "personal space." The research indicates to the degree that people who are crowded together can cooperate and control the circumstances of their crowding, their experience of stress diminishes.[45] Sheldon Cohen and Neil Weinstein observe that noise as unwanted sound is a psychological concept.[46] Unpredictable and uncontrollable noise causes stress rather than just noise itself. For example, some people prefer to listen to music at a high decibel level, while others in the immediate vicinity may resent the noise that is imposed on them.

The most frequently mentioned neighborhood problem is excessive noise. Barking dogs rank high on the list, as do loud music and loud children. Community noise research indicates that people do not adapt well to neighborhood noise. Surprisingly, longitudinal research suggests that the longer one is exposed to excessive noise the more disturbing one finds it. Anger and anxiety are common psychological reactions to prolonged, unwanted, loud noise.[47]

Workplace Stress

The sources of stress in the workplace include physical, psychological, and organizational factors, including tempo, crowding, and noise. Indeed, broaching the subject of technology and stress suggests a discussion of the workplace. A large amount of research has been conducted on workplace stress caused by technology.[48]

The intensity of work has been increasing in recent decades.[49] This is due both to pressure on employees to keep pace with technology and to management techniques designed to make employees more efficient. There is considerable overlap between machine technology and management technique because the former is now a component of the latter and because both are forms of technology. Workplace stress now affects blue-collar workers, white-collar workers, and managers. Management technique has been turned on management itself. Indeed, workplace stress may now be greater among managers than among lower-echelon workers.[50]

One of the earliest forms of job stress is the alienation inherent in the horizontal and vertical division of labor. The horizontal division of labor refers to the creation of a series of specialized tasks for what was originally a unified accomplishment. Specialized tasks can be given to different individuals. The result is that no one person experiences the satisfaction of creating a product in its entirety. The vertical division of labor refers to the separation of knowledge from the experiences of the person performing the task. The abstract knowledge is embedded in a machine, a manager, or a software program to the effect that the worker becomes a servant to the objectified knowledge.[51] These kinds of workplace stress have been recognized since at least the nineteenth century by a number of writers, including Karl Marx. Although recent efforts to overcome the vertical division of labor have included giving workers more say in modifying work procedures, the subordination of workers at all levels to the computer offsets these gains.

The time Americans spend working has been increasing for white-collar professionals and some unionized employees (when the economy is strong). More than 25 million people work at least forty-nine hours a week; 15 million people work between fifty and sixty hours a week; 11 million report that they work at least sixty hours a week. Not all of this occurs in the workplace, however. The job has forced its way into the home and the weekend; moreover, commuting time and travel time are increasing.[52] One is never quite not at work.

The workplace has shrunk by 25 percent to 50 percent in the last decade. Office workers are imprisoned in cubicles that afford little privacy. The cubicles are housed in "bullpens," large open areas that maximize the opportunity for surveillance. Still others have only "virtual offices" and only use a real office when necessary.[53] Crowding destroys privacy and sense of self, whereas the virtual office reaffirms how transitory and expendable the employee has become.

The growing use of temporary employees and consultants and the constant threat of downsizing reinforce the latter point. Far from being a product of economic hard times, such practices increased in America in the 1990s, a period of great economic prosperity. In 1998, downsizing corporations resulted in the loss of 677,000 jobs. Whether mistaken or not, many high-ranking managers came to believe that these practices played a critical role in sustaining this prosperity. Mergers often result in downsizing as a way of indicating to stockholders that the company will do whatever it takes to maximize short-term profits. The use of "contingent" workers, temporaries and consultants, reduces the overall cost of benefits to employees; moreover, it gives the company maximum flexibility in the efficient use of labor. Electronics and computer companies are among the heaviest users of "contingent" employees in part because the speed and cost of innovation is so high for them. Some contingent workers remain temporary for so long that they refer to themselves as "permatemps."[54]

As the competition for profits increases and the company's loyalty to its employees diminishes, there is a marked increase in rude, hostile, and bullying behavior.[55] Even under the best circumstances bureaucracies are an amoral form of organization; but when job insecurity and competition become pervasive, employee relationships become fully political.[56] One manager discovered a bright side to the threat of psychological violence: "Fear can be a powerful management tool."[57]

Fear assumes many forms, however, as managers have been quick to discover. Using the work team to force employees to keep pace with one another is sometimes referred to as "lean production," but others more aptly call it "management by stress." The Toyota version of lean production involves an overhead visual display that represents each worker's workstation by a rectangular box. When a worker falls behind the rest of the assembly line and needs assistance, she pulls a cord that lights up the corresponding box on the visual display. Only if the light remains on more than a minute does the assembly line shut down. In a traditional assembly line the object is to keep the line operating continuously at a predetermined pace. Management by stress demands that the assembly line be sped up so that workers can only keep pace by working harder or improving their work technique. "The ideal is for the system to run with all stations oscillating between lights on and lights off."[58] When workers, who are encouraged to help make the assembly line more efficient, improve the speed of the line, managers increase the pace of production. Consequently, workers can never relax with a comfortable pace but face the continuing anxiety of an ever increasing work pace. "Democratic participation" in the workplace comes at a heavy price.

White-collar employees too are working longer and faster. A middle manager at Levi Strauss suggests that each employee is now doing the work that two and a half employees previously did. E-mail, phone calls, and faxes force employees to interrupt their work. A 1999 business survey found that the average office employee sent or received 201 messages daily.[59] Even if some of the messages permit employees to work efficiently, there is no provision for the time spent sending and receiving messages.

The widespread use of the computer allows workers' performance to be monitored. Managers are able to keep employees under more or less total surveillance with computerized work. Moreover, to the extent that companies employ public relations and group activities to manipulate employees into identifying with the company, total institutions are created.[60] The company becomes a home away from home, a family perhaps, but a dysfunctional one marred by competition and fear.

So far we have examined how the workplace is organized to maximize employee productivity and create overall organizational efficiency. How do employees react to these stressful arrangements? What are the consequences of long-term exposure to stress?

First, employees perceive that they are being overworked. Frazer agrees that this perception is accurate: "People are working ten or twelve hours a day. They're working through their lunch hours, during their commutes to and from the office, in squeezed-in spare moments during their evening hours, and whenever else they absolutely need to on weekends and holidays." The International Survey Research Corporation discovered in the mid-1990s that 44 percent of those surveyed in corporations thought that their workloads were too heavy.[61]

Employees also perceive that they have lost even more control over their work in recent years. Employees who operate computers for long periods of time complain that the computer eventually controls them. In other words, this common complaint expresses the intuition they have become "extensions of the machine."[62] Even more important than what the computer allows us to do is what it does *for* us and *to* us. The computer, like all machines at a certain level of proficiency, "de-skills" employees and forces them to work at its pace.

Even when employees are part of work teams that permit workers to modify the work process, some understand that the work team is being used to maximize productivity and thus increase the pace of work. At all levels of the organization employees sense that an increase in work time, work pace, and work load means a loss of control of their job.

The acceleration of time as the pace of work increases produces in some workers irritation and impatience with the constant interruptions of their work and with fellow employees, customers, and even their computers when they are too slow in making a decision. A recent study indicated that any computer response time more than 1.5 seconds made employees impatient.[63]

The reality of downsizing and temporary employment results in widespread fear among employees.[64] It makes them less sure about the stability of their jobs and may even lead to a contempt for temporary workers, who are seen as potential competitors and may even symbolize the future of work. As one employee put it, trust has evaporated with widespread downsizing and the increasing use of contingency labor. Sometimes anxiety about maintaining one's job leads to emotional detachment from work. One middle management bank employee facing impending corporate downsizing felt so helpless that she distanced herself emotionally from the anxiety of fellow employees.[65]

Emotional isolation can also result from the use of the computer.[66] Communication by e-mail does not satisfy the employee's need for personal contact. A friendly workplace ranks high among the qualities employees look for in a job. As we have seen previously, heavy use of the computer results in loneliness and depression.

What are the psychological and physiological consequences of experiencing undue stress? And how pervasive is it? A 1999 study estimated the cost of workplace stress in the United States as $200 billion, a large part of which is due to absenteeism.[67] Between 1980 and 1990 worker compensation claims related to stress increased 300 percent.[68] Stress-related problems appear to be highest among workers whose performance is monitored.[69] One Japanese study found that over 70 percent of Japanese workers felt mentally exhausted after work.[70] Indeed, the Japanese have a term, "death by overwork," to describe the extreme manifestation of this pathology. It is even more prevalent among managers than among lower level white-collar workers and blue-collar workers.[71]

The consequences of long-term exposure to excessive stress include fear, insecurity, mental exhaustion, emotional detachment, loneliness, and even depression. Moreover, there is a correlation between stress and headaches, stomachaches, ulcers, high blood pressure, colorectal cancer, and miscarriage.[72] The irrational pursuit of efficiency is producing an emotionally crippled and perhaps physically disabled labor force.

The Technological Personality as "Stimulus Shield"

The consequences of stress are mitigated to a certain extent by the technological personality. Humans have learned to "internalize" some stressful stimuli and in so doing have adapted to them. The concept of the "stimulus shield" as applied to technology is so important to my argument that we will look at Wolfgang Schivelbusch's seminal idea in some detail.[73]

The theme of his book *The Railway Journey* is how the railroad, specifically travel by rail, affected the perception of time and space. In his view this is only one part of how industrialization in the nineteenth century influenced the human psyche. Schivelbusch demonstrates how railway travel created panoramic vision. The velocity of the train made it impossible for the traveler to intensely study the landscape. Now perception became extensive: one viewed as much as possible in the brief time allotted by the speed of the train. One learned to take in the entire landscape at once rather than consecutively.[74]

Schivelbusch's discussion of the stimulus shield as a way of normalizing a technology that produces fear and anxiety allows us to see stress in a new light. Railway travelers, he argues, created new ways of perceiving and behaving that allowed them to forget their fear of train travel. The size and speed of trains frightened people; accidents appeared more imminent and more deadly. The train manufacturers tried to mitigate the fear that trains would crash by minimizing the jolts and noise that suggested the possibility of a train wreck; moreover, compartment decor created an elegant atmosphere that distracted travelers from their anxiety about a train wreck. Reading on trains almost became mandatory; it distracted passengers from their fear. Finally, panoramic vision represented a way of internalizing the speed of the train, which suggested a possible train wreck.

Schivelbusch explains that the higher the technology, the more catastrophic its destruction. Historically, catastrophes were the result of natural forces such as a floods, which could destroy human products from the *outside*. A higher-level technological object, like a train, is destroyed from the *inside*, by means of its own power. Because natural catastrophes were rare occurrences and external to humans, nature was not as frightening. Higher-level technologies, however, were catastrophes waiting to happen. It is one thing to be riding in a horse and buggy with the distant possibility of a tornado, and quite another to be riding on a train that could at any time explode. Schivelbusch also notes that the higher the level of the technology, the more "denaturalized" human consciousness becomes. When that "denaturalized" consciousness collapses in the case of a technological accident, the psychic shock is much greater than in the instance of a natural catastrophe.[75]

The denaturalized consciousness includes the idea of the stimulus shield, a term taken from Freud. It is more or less synonymous, Schivelbusch argues, with Simmel's term "intelligence." For Freud, new and strong stimuli, such as train travel or flying in an airplane, tend to produce a "skin layer of consciousness," or a "thicker layer of skin," so that the stimuli become less threatening. In other words, the observer "internalizes" the stimuli, becomes acclimated to them, dulls them, so that it would take novel stimuli to once again frighten him. Simmel's comparable idea is that when faced with pervasive and intense stimuli, such as living and working in a large city, the individual reacts intellectually rather than emotionally to them. This emotional indifference is a way of protecting the individual from emotional upheaval and exhaustion. The panoramic vision is a perfect illustration of the internalization of changes in time and space that train travel caused.[76]

A corollary of this is that once the individual internalizes the stimuli, previous stimuli are hardly recognizable. Schivelbusch explains, "Once the traveler had reorganized his perception so that it became panoramic, he no longer had an eye for the impressions of, say, a coach trip."[77] The previously satisfying stimuli no longer register with the observer who now requires greater stimulation.

Let us now apply the concept of stimulus shield to life in the late twentieth and early twenty-first centuries. Some of the writers I will draw on have intuited Schivelbusch's idea. The following discussion applies mainly to the computer and the mass media. Craig Brod has observed that workers who use computers sometimes display irritation with people and machines that do not perform quickly enough. Brod perceptively notes that in such cases the "worker internalizes the rapid, instant access mode of computer operations."[78]

Jerry Mander notes that the mass media (including the computer) have sped up our perceptual and nervous systems.[79] Consequently, many of us are "bored" with a slower pace of life, time alone to read and think, time to be introspective. Because reality is in the media and the computer, to be alone is to be out of touch, to become fantastic. We cannot temporarily withdraw from the company of others to better prepare to rejoin this company later; to conform we must be encapsulated in the media. In Schivelbusch's terms we find it difficult to return to the slower stimuli of reading and thinking. Some researchers have discovered that "understimulation" can be experienced as stress.[80]

Attention deficit disorder and hyperactivity are only the extreme manifestations of our internalization of the rapid movement of media images and sounds. Jane Healy has studied both disorders and sees their relationship to heavy television viewing and prolonged playing of video and computer games.[81] Attention deficit disorder is independent of hyperactivity, but they sometimes occur together. Both have been diagnosed as forms of learning disability. Attention deficit disorder entails the inability to maintain attention and concentrate on a specific task. Hyperactivity applies to those who cannot concentrate and also have trouble sitting still; their bodies must be in constant motion.[82] Healy cites research on the brain and central nervous system suggesting that overexposure to the mass media and computer may prevent synapses from forming properly in the left hemisphere of the brain so that the ability to read, write, and think is stunted.[83] Someone who lacks facility in language does not understand much of what goes on in school and experiences wandering attention. This mimics the media visual, which moves rapidly from one image to another, from one topic to another.

The ability to read, write, and think is generally declining.[84] The problem is not merely too much television or too much video and computer games but the low quality of conversation and what is read. As Healy notes, students are not expected often enough to read complex sentences and struggle with complex thoughts.[85] Moreover, there has been a dramatic decline in the level of discourse in the media, in textbooks, and in the books most adults read.[86] Given the fast pace of life in a technological society and the rapid movement of images in the media and video and computer games, it is understandable that we have all become mildly hyperactive and all suffer from attention deficit disorder to some extent. Hyperactivity and attention deficit disorder are this century's stimulus shields.

The impact of the media (including the computer) includes loss of memory, personal thought, and feeling. Memory is an integral part of one's existence; it is a product of one's relationship to reality defined by culture and placed into the context of one's entire life.[87] Memory tends to be centered on key events and people that have acquired a certain symbolic quality. There is neither past nor future in the media, only the present.[88] The media aestheticize reality and turn life into a spectacle to be enjoined now. There is no need for memory, at least long-term memory, when one lives exclusively in and for the moment.

Visual images have a largely emotional impact on us.[89] When we watch television, the activity in the left hemisphere of the brain is about what it is when we are asleep.[90] Today adults as well as children spend much more time watching the media and playing video and computer games than they do reading. What reading they do tends not to be serious.[91] The result is catastrophic. Healy observes that "professionals report that children in classrooms seem to be thinking and learning in increasingly more nonsequential and visual ways."[92] Consequently there is a decline in logical thought and critical reflection. The image-oriented individual is more readily influenced by propaganda, advertising, and public relations. Healy reports that the use of music with a heavy beat "blocks the capacity for thinking." Children may be learning "to swaddle their brains in sensation-dulling music as an escape from excesses of stimulation in everyday life."[93] The music-addicted mind functions as a stimulus shield.

Finally, Brod discusses the anxiety the computer creates for its users. They tend to make one of two responses: a "struggle to accept the computer" or "overidentification" with it. Those who embrace the computer and make it the center of their lives suffer the "loss of the capacity to feel and to relate to others."[94] In other words, they become like the computer.

The mass media and the computer have led to a loss of memory, thought, and feeling. We are becoming more like machines, which possess none of these capabilities. Our stimulus shield allows us to internalize certain machines—the media and the computer.

The Theory of the Technological Personality

In chapter 1, we saw that the technological personality—the aggressively cheerful, garrulous, mildly hyperactive *outer* personality—compensated for the lonely, fearful *inner* personality. But the technological personality serves other purposes as well. The technological personality with its hyperactivity and loss of attention, memory, thought, and feeling internalizes both the tempo and synchronicity of a technological civilization and the machine itself. We engage in frantic activity and frantic communication without much thought or feeling. As Ellul succinctly puts it, in a technological civilization reflex supplants reflection.[95]

All this frantic activity and communication serve to distract the technological personality from the loneliness and fear that the inner personality ex-

periences. Yet these distractions are only superficially and temporarily successful, for the technological personality reinforces the experience of loneliness. The stress that technology directly creates is qualitatively different from
the kind it generates by indirectly making human relationships more abstract, impersonal, vague, and competitive. The technological personality is
not a stimulus shield to loneliness, as it will subsequently become evident.
All of us differ in the extent to which our personalities resemble the technological personality. The individual whose personality is close to the technological personality simultaneously experiences less technological stress and
more loneliness.

In the introduction, I mentioned Ellul's great insight that in a technological civilization everything is an imitation of technology or a compensation
for its impact or both. The technological personality perfectly illustrates this.
As stimulus shield, the technological personality *imitates* technology by internalizing it. The technological personality *compensates* for the inner lonely
personality (an indirect result of technology) by extroverted cheerfulness.

Notes

1. See, for example, Gary Evans, ed., *Environmental Stress* (New York: Cambridge
University Press, 1982); and Willem Vanderburg, *The Labyrinth of Technology*
(Toronto: Toronto University Press, 2000).

2. Gary Evans, "General Introduction," in *Environmental Stress*, 8–9.

3. Andrew Baum, Jerome Singer, and Carlene Baum, "Stress and the Environment," in *Environmental Stress*, 16–17.

4. Baum, Singer, and Baum, "Stress and the Environment," 17.

5. Baum, Singer, and Baum, "Stress and the Environment," 26–31.

6. Baum, Singer, and Baum, "Stress and the Environment," 20–21.

7. Baum, Singer, and Baum, "Stress and the Environment," 34.

8. Robert Levine, *A Geography of Time* (New York: Basic, 1997), 3.

9. Levine, *Geography of Time*, 25.

10. Levine, *Geography of Time*, 24.

11. Jeremy Rifkin, *The End of Work* (New York: Putnam, 1995), 186.

12. Levine, *Geography of Time*, 20–21.

13. Staffan Linder, *The Harried Leisured Class* (New York: Columbia University
Press, 1970), chap. 1.

14. Levine, *Geography of Time*, 22–24.

15. James Gleick, *Faster* (New York: Pantheon, 1999), 10.

16. Jerry Mander, *In the Absence of the Sacred* (San Francisco: Sierra Club Books,
1991), 85.

17. Jacques Ellul, *The Humiliation of the Word*, trans. Joyce Hanks (Grand Rapids, Mich.: Eerdmans, 1985), 147.

18. Linder, *Harried Leisure Class*, 79.

19. On this point there is a plethora of materials. See, for example, Richard Stivers, *Technology as Magic* (New York: Continuum, 1999), chap. 4.

20. Daniel Boorstin, *The Image: A Guide to Pseudo-Events in America* (New York: Harper & Row, 1961), chap. 3.

21. Arlie Hochschild, *The Time Bind* (New York: Metropolitan Books, 1997).

22. Hochschild, *Time Bind*, 45–52.

23. David Brooks, "The Organization Kid," *Atlantic*, April 2001, 40–54.

24. Linder, *Harried Leisure Class*.

25. Jacques Ellul, *The Technological Bluff*, trans. Geoffrey Bromiley (Grand Rapids, Mich.: Eerdmans, 1990), 95.

26. Jacques Ellul, *The Technological System*, trans. Joachim Neugroschel (New York: Continuum, 1980).

27. Max Horkheimer and Theodor Adorno, *Dialectic of Enlightenment*, trans. John Cumming (New York: Herder & Herder, 1972).

28. Linder, *Harried Leisure Class*, 64–67.

29. Walter Kerr, *The Decline of Pleasure* (New York: Simon & Schuster, 1965).

30. Jacques Ellul, *The Technological Society*, trans. John Wilkinson (New York: Vintage, 1964), 421.

31. Milan Kundera, *Slowness* (New York: HarperCollins, 1996), 2; see also Jean Baudrillard, "The Ecstasy of Communication," in *The Anti-Aesthetic* (Seattle: Bay, 1983), 126–33.

32. Ellul, *Technological Society*, 422–26.

33. The following discussion is taken from Ellul, *Technological Bluff*, 329–32.

34. Cynthia Crossen, *Tainted Truth* (New York: Simon & Schuster, 1994).

35. Jacques Ellul, *The Political Illusion*, trans. Konrad Kellen (New York: Vintage, 1967), 8–24.

36. Tom Shachtman, *The Inarticulate Society* (New York: Tree, 1995), 100.

37. Neil Postman, *Amusing Ourselves to Death* (New York: Viking, 1985), 136–37.

38. Tzvetan Todorov, "The Two Principles of Narrative" in *Genres in Discourse*, trans. Catherine Porter (New York: Cambridge University Press, 1990), 27–38.

39. George Gerbner and Larry Gross, "The Scary World of TV's Heavy Viewer," *Psychology Today*, April 1976, 41–45, 89.

40. Ellul, *Humiliation of the Word*, 209.

41. Ellul, *Humiliation of the Word*, 121–28.

42. Don Delillo, *Mao II* (New York: Viking, 1991), 24.

43. Robert Kraut and Vicki Lundmark, "The Internet Paradox: A Social Technology That Reduces Social Involvement and Psychological Well-Being?" *American Psychologist* 53 (1998): 1017–31, as cited in Clifford Stoll, *High-Tech Heretic* (New York: Doubleday, 1999), 198–201.

44. Vanderburg, *Labyrinth of Technology*, 377–80.

45. Yakov Epstein, "Crowding Stress and Human Behavior," in *Environmental Stress*, 137–41.

46. Sheldon Cohen and Neil Weinstein, "Nonauditory Effects of Noise on Behavior and Health," in *Environmental Stress*, 46.

47. Cohen and Weinstein, "Nonauditory Effects, 56–60.

48. See Vanderburg, *Labyrinth of Technology*, chap. 10, for a review and interpretation of this research.

49. Vanderburg, *Labyrinth of Technology*, 324.

50. The issue of stress among managers has been profitably explored by Jill Fraser, *White-Collar Sweatshop* (New York: Norton, 2001).

51. Vanderburg, *Labyrinth of Technology*, 328–33.

52. Fraser, *White-Collar Sweatshop*, 20–27.

53. Fraser, *White-Collar Sweatshop*, 35–36.

54. Fraser, *White-Collar Sweatshop*, 135–45.

55. Fraser, *White-Collar Sweatshop*, 32–33.

56. See Robert Jackall, *Moral Mazes* (New York: Oxford University Press, 1988), for an excellent discussion of the moral and political environment of the modern corporation.

57. Fraser, *White-Collar Sweatshop*, 32; see also David Gordon, *Fat and Mean* (New York: Free Press, 1996), chap. 6.

58. Mike Parker and Jane Slaughter, "Management by Stress," *Technology Review*, October 1988, 39.

59. Fraser, *White-Collar Sweatshop*, 21, 82.

60. Martin Kenney and Richard Florida, *Beyond Mass Production* (New York: Oxford University Press, 1993), 271.

61. Fraser, *White-Collar Sweatshop*, 135–45.

62. Craig Brod, *Technostress* (Reading: Addison-Wesley, 1984), 44–49.

63. Brod, *Technostress*, 43.

64. Fraser, *White-Collar Sweatshop*, 135–45.

65. Fraser, *White-Collar Sweatshop*, 169–70.

66. Brod, *Technostress*, 49–50.

67. Frazer, *White-Collar Sweatshop*, 36.

68. Rifkin, *End of Work*, 190.

69. Barbara Garson, *The Electronic Sweatshop* (New York: Norton, 1988), 113.

70. Vanderburg, *Labyrinth of Technology*, 324.

71. Kennedy and Florida, *Beyond Mass Production*, 264–65.

72. Gunilla Bradley, *Computers and the Psychosocial Work Environment*, trans. Struan Robertson (London: Taylor & Francis, 1989), 147; Frazer, *White-Collar Sweatshop*, 37–38.

73. Wolfgang Schivelbusch, *The Railway Journey* (Berkeley: University of California Press, 1986).

74. Schivelbusch, *Railway Journey*, chap. 4.

75. Schivelbusch, *Railway Journey*, chap. 8.

76. Schivelbusch, *Railway Journey*, chap. 10.

77. Schivelbusch, *Railway Journey*, 165.

78. Brod, *Technostress*, 43.

79. Mander, *In the Absence of the Sacred*, 86.

80. Bradley, *Computers and the Psychosocial*, 86.

81. Jane Healy, *Endangered Minds* (New York: Touchstone Books, 1991), chaps. 7–8.

82. Healy, *Endangered Minds*, 139.

83. Healy, *Endangered Minds*, chaps. 10–11.

84. Stivers, *Technology as Magic*, chap. 2.

85. Healy, *Endangered Minds*, chap. 11.

86. Stivers, *Technology as Magic*, 44–48.

87. Ellul, *Humiliation of the Word*, 121–23.

88. Ellul, *Humiliation of the Word*, chap. 3.

89. E. H. Gombrich, "The Visual Image," *Scientific American*, September 1972, 82–96.

90. Jerry Mander, *Four Arguments for the Elimination of Television* (New York: Quill, 1978), 205–11.

91. Stivers, *Technology as Magic*, 44–45.

92. Healy, *Endangered Minds*, 132.

93. Healy, *Endangered Minds*, 175.

94. Brod, *Technostress*, 16–18.

95. Ellul, *Technological Society*, chap. 5.

~

CHAPTER THREE

Cultural and Psychological Conflict

The technological personality does not act as an effective stimulus shield against loneliness. If anything, the technological personality, which is fragmented, only exacerbates the loneliness for which it is a screen. Loneliness is a consequence of ambiguous relationships with others. Uncertainty about and unresolvable conflicts with others in turn result in internal conflicts, which serve to exacerbate the loneliness. The vicious circle is that those who suffer acutely from loneliness are least capable of establishing deep, lasting relationships with others.

Ambiguous relationships and psychological conflicts are related to cultural ambiguity and cultural contradictions. Indeed, the erosion of cultural meaning and cultural contradictions are responsible for ambiguous human relationships and our chronic conflicts with others. Although only more serious forms of loneliness deserve to be termed neurotic, as Karen Horney observes, the distinction between the normal and the neurotic today has become blurred.[1]

In this chapter, drawing principally on the work of J. H. van den Berg and Karen Horney, I will set forth a theory of neurosis that establishes its social causes. Van den Berg would rename neurosis "sociosis" and notes that "no one is neurotic unless made so by society. A neurosis is an individual's reaction to the conflicting and complicating demands made by society."[2] In other words, neurosis is a social "disease" before it is a psychological one. Support for van den Berg's contention is the fact that prior to the eighteenth century there was no character neurosis, that is, chronic as opposed to situational neurosis.[3] Along the same lines, Stanley Diamond argues that schizophrenia is virtually unknown in primitive societies; it is a product of civilization, especially modern civilization.[4] Therefore it is necessary to specify what changes in the organization of society gave rise to widespread neurosis and increased psychosis.

The idea of a "sick society" was seemingly discredited in the early twentieth century both because the concept was vague and because most psychologists and psychiatrists did not think in sociological terms. At the same time, most sociologists were ignorant of the psychiatric and psychological literature and had their own version of social psychology that concentrated on small groups rather than the larger society. What was needed was what van den Berg and Horney respectively provided, a sociological theory of psychopathology. As insightful as their work is, it still needs to be put into the context of what in their day was only just emerging—a technological civilization. The cultural contradictions that Horney and van den Berg addressed as the source of neurosis need to be reinterpreted accordingly.

J. H. van den Berg

J. H. van den Berg is both a psychiatrist and a clinical psychologist; more specifically, he is an advocate of historical psychology. The latter involves the study of sociological structures and their impact on personality and psychological processes. Van den Berg's theory of neurosis is thus both historical and sociological.

The first cause of neurosis is anomie. In the late nineteenth century, Emile Durkheim gave the term its more or less accepted sociological meanings. In *The Division of Labor in Society*, Durkheim used anomie to refer to the lack of moral guidance in the relations between social functions and between positions in the social structure (e.g., labor and management). Anomie represented a "pathological" condition of industrialized capitalism, in particular, large industry and large markets. Economic relationships became vague and confused under industrialized capitalism because they were no longer guided by tradition and fixed status.

In his later work *Suicide*, Durkheim altered the meaning of anomie so that it becomes a social psychological concept having to do with the failure of social groups to morally regulate the individual.[5] Van den Berg extends and refines the earlier version of Durkheim's concept by situating it in a larger historical and cultural context. The emphasis is on relationships: both between groups and within groups. Morality does not just regulate the relationships between individuals but also those between groups.

There is no morality without some kind of authority embedded in a social hierarchy.

In *Divided Existence and Complex Society*, van den Berg examines the emergence of pluralism in Western Europe in the late eighteenth century.[6] In the form most relevant to the study of neurosis, pluralism refers to disintegration of social structure, that is, to the erosion of the boundaries between social groups, whether vertical or horizontal. In traditional societies everyone had an inherited status of age, sex, occupation, family, and class. Moreover, all knew what prescribed relationship existed between their group and another group (e.g., between men and women, between the old and the young, between hunters and farmers). In short, a social structure divides society into distinct groups, only to reunite them through a set of mutual responsibilities and obligations. When the clear division between groups and statuses becomes vague, pluralism ensues.[7] Society becomes a loose collection of groups that have no established relationships to one another and little actual interaction.

Related to the pluralism of society is the type and size of groups to which people belong. We typically belong to fewer small informal groups, such as a neighborhood group, and they tend to be ephemeral. Instead we belong to a more or less random collection of large secondary groups.[8] The voluntary associations seem innumerable and almost infinite in theme. Political groups, charitable groups, unions, professional organizations, clubs and recreational groups abound. Daniel Boorstin refers to the rise of consumption communities, people whose sole commonality is the product or service they use (e.g., those who frequent McDonald's).[9] Our relationship to others in such secondary groups, apart from the stated purpose, tends to be uncertain. The group's hold on the individual, moreover, is specific to its function. These large secondary groups only relate to one part of the self in contradistinction to smaller primary groups that appeal to the whole self.

The relationship between groups and between the individual and the group is vague. The individual only possesses a unified self when her relationship to others is clearly demarcated. The unity of the individual is coterminous with the unity of the community. As we have seen, unity implies differentiation; it likewise suggests complementarity. The group of men and the group of women exist in a complementary relationship to each other, for example. Although one has a variety of statuses and groups based on age, sex, and occupation, one knows how each group is expected to relate to its complement. Moreover, the various groups do not make contradictory demands on the individual. To be a member of the group of women and a member of the group of old people does not require a different self in each instance. The same self, in which being a woman and being old are integrated, is present in each interaction with members of other groups. When the various groups are not integrated into complementary relationships, they may become special interest groups that make contradictory demands on the individual. For example, the interests of women conflict with those of old people in the competition for scarce resources. This is the situation today. Consequently, we now have multiple selves, as many selves as groups to which we belong, even as many selves as individuals we know reasonably well. Harry Stack Sullivan termed this phenomenon "paratactic" experience.[10] Each relationship with others creates a different synthesis: with Bob, I am Dick (Bob); with Jim, I am Dick (Jim); with Frank, Dick (Frank). I am a different person each time, for I have no unitary self. Part of my self is manifest in each interaction; the other parts (or selves) remain hidden. Those who are not neurotic (the line between the normal and the neurotic is blurred, as Karen Horney reminds us) are able to manage their multiple selves without undue difficulty. The neurotic, van den Berg observes, becomes lost in a maze of selves. Sociologist Pitirim Sorokin was the first to refer to neurosis as a "conflict of social egos."[11]

The most general cause of pluralism, according to van den Berg, is anomie, as we have previously seen. Anomie refers both to the ambiguous relationship between groups in society and to the group's inability to integrate the individual into itself. In other words, the failure of moral integration at all levels of society.

In a more general sense, the integration of groups and individuals involves four factors. First, one belongs to various groups (e.g., age, sex, occupation) without having to gain admittance. One naturally or automatically belongs to the groups appropriate to one's positions in society. No one is isolated. Second, the various social groups are small, permitting one to have personal knowledge and ties to virtually everyone in the group. Third, the speed of change is quite slow so that customs and traditions appear to be permanent. Fourth, all sectors of social existence—work and play, religion and politics, nature and society—are integrated into a meaningful, coherent totality. Life may not be pleasant but it makes sense.[12]

What gave rise to anomie in the late eighteenth century? The most important factor was a decline in the belief in God and in the certainty that moral principles as derived from God are objectively true. Religion and moral values were gradually becoming subjective but retained their importance in relation to the individual. Increasingly reason, especially science, defined what was objectively true. Adam Smith perfectly expressed this view in the late eighteenth century in A Theory of Moral Sentiments: Religion and morality were part of the private sector of life, whereas the economy and the state dominated the public sector. When religion and morality began to lose their hold on society as a whole, science and technology, which can only inform us about and control empirical reality, were not up to the task of integrating society.

Anomie, however, becomes manifest in different sectors of society at different times. For instance, the sector of spirituality or sex and aggression can become isolated from the other sectors of society.

Isolation and ambiguity give rise to what Freud mistakenly called the "unconscious." Unawareness is a more apt term. Van den Berg suggests that the unconscious is a communicative phenomenon, the "index of nearness or remoteness in one's relationship with other people."[13] To the extent that our interaction with others is not based on mutual trust and transparency, which only occurs when a society is well integrated, their consciousness is our unconsciousness, and our consciousness is their unconsciousness. There is no unconsciousness when each person is aware of where he stands in relation to others and what the societal expectations are in regard to them. The consciousness of the individual is identical to the consciousness of the entire community.

The unconscious of others extends to oneself, for our own sense of self depends in part on how others respond to us. For example, if no one laughs at my jokes, I will not think of myself as humorous. When others respond to us in a vague or insincere way, our sense of self becomes ambiguous. One then becomes, as it were, unconscious to oneself.

Van den Berg demonstrates that Freud's apparent discovery that repressed sexuality was the basis of the unconscious was a historical accident—a product of the Victorian period. In the amalgam of groups belonging to public life, sexuality was absent; it was a taboo subject. In the lives of married people (and their older sons), sexuality was present. The middle-class woman was a member of a family, friendship groups, and a church. These groups left her unaware of sex. The repressed sexuality of the middle-class woman was actually an unawareness of sex that sometimes had hysterical consequences when she was first confronted with a man's sexuality.

The anomic isolation of sexuality extended to aggression and all bodily functions. Later anomie entered the sector of religion insofar as religion was relegated to private life. Western societies have become increasing secularized, at least in regard to their Judeo-Christian heritage. More people have at best a superficial knowledge of their parents' religion. Van den Berg maintains that spirituality was the most important sector of society after that of sexuality to experience anomic isolation.[14] To a great extent it has supplanted sexuality as a major source of anomie. Today anomie extends to all sectors of society, in other words, to society as a whole.[15]

And yet anomie has changed its face. Anomic isolation used to mean that an entire sector of society was left unconscious, and consequently certain individuals (e.g., unmarried Victorian women) were left unaware of that sector. Van den Berg acknowledges that today sex is universally present in the media; no one could be unaware of it.[16] But this awareness is superficial; it is not normative, at least in the traditional sense of the term. Public opinion acts as an ersatz morality, but it is ephemeral, hardly providing any stability in one's relationship to others.[17] The media have recently turned their attention to spirituality and have even linked it to health and longevity. Once again, a superficial awareness ensues. There is no true normative direction to that sector of life. The media have made us aware of everything, but we still remain unconscious of one another, especially now that anomie has spread to society as a whole. Without normative regulation of the relationship between groups and between the group and the individual, interpersonal relations remain vague and potentially dangerous.

The single most important form of anomie is that in regard to spirituality. For as van den Berg observes, whoever has a deep relationship with God will never be lonely. Even if one's relationship to others is ambiguous and one experiences isolation one still has a clearly-defined relationship to God and thus is not lonely. The chief symptom of neurosis is pervasive loneliness and a related fear of others.

More than any other form of anomie, the anomic isolation of spirituality is responsible for a cultural emphasis on equality. The norm of equality, which itself is a consequence of anomie, reinforces and deepens it (anomie). What van den Berg means by the norm of equality is not the equality of a universal love or the equality of an idealistic socialism, but a descriptive norm that everyone is actually equal (e.g., in ability, accomplishment, experience, and wisdom). We are all more or less identical. This norm of equality suggests more than that humans should be treated equally but that they are homogeneous. The norm of equality removes all vestiges of authority; moreover, it makes us ambivalent about recognizing the actual differences among us. It is the contradiction between real inequality and the norm of equality that allows anomie to make its presence more pervasive.

The descriptive norm of equality is born out of loneliness and fear. Those who are lonely and fearful come together as equals for consolation and protection. Van den Berg notes that the modern obsession with chitchat, talk about nothing in particular, "group-centered" talk, is a consequence of loneliness. Traditional peoples talked much less, and their talk was for the most part "task-centered." Task-centered talk was hierarchical, that is, based on authority; group-centered talk makes everyone equal.[18]

The contradictions between inequality and the norm of equality continue the work that anomie began—to make human relationships vague, insincere, and competitive. David Riesman observed that the peer group in an other-directed era was composed of members who were unconsciously "antagonistic cooperators."[19] The norm of equality deepens the cultural chaos of anomie. It is not just groups and sectors of society that suffer from anomic isolation but each individual. The neurotic, van den Berg asserts, is the one among us who gets "lost in the maze" of insincere and vague relationships.[20]

Karen Horney

Karen Horney was a psychoanalyst who disagreed with Freud on a number of issues, including his views on women and on repressed sexuality as the basis of neurosis, but was nonetheless appreciative of a number of his insights. Unlike van den Berg, she never rejected the reality of the Freudian unconscious but only its content. Horney appears to have been the first modern theorist of psychopathology to stress sociological factors in the genesis of neurosis.[21] Although Horney's sociological description is much briefer than van den Berg's, her discussion of its impact on the individual neurotic is much more detailed. For Horney, the sociological question concerns the "cultural circumstances that create emotional isolation, hostility, insecurity, and fear."[22] The neurotic experiences unusually strong inner and outer (with others) conflict as a consequence.

The various conflicts of the neurotic have their counterpart (as well as indirect cause) in what she referred to as cultural contradictions: specific cultural contradictions determine the form of neurotic conflicts. Horney identified three major contradictions in American culture, the first existing between individual success and brotherly love. As she observes, to pursue success vigorously is to use other people as means to that goal. To take the ethic of love seriously means to subordinate one's success to the needs of others. The second contradiction exists between the constant stimulation of our needs by advertising and the great difficulty most people have in satisfying these needs. The frustration may ensue either from one's inability to purchase consumer goods or the fact that they do not satisfy the needs for which they were created. Hence we are trapped in vicious circle of frustration in which our ever escalating "needs" have less and less chance of being satisfied. The third contradiction exists between individual freedom and the myriad social determinisms that strip us of our limited freedom. For example, we are free to choose among a variety of consumer goods, but not to decide whether or not to become consumers. Consumerism is a technological and economic imperative. Perhaps never before have people talked so much about freedom even as the power of the state, the corporation, and technology over the individual grows.[23]

Strictly speaking, only the first is a true cultural contradiction. Individual success and love are both espoused by American culture. The latter two contradictions involve a conflict between a cultural value and the way social reality negates it. Hence the satisfaction of artificially created desires and the value of freedom are next to impossible to realize in practice. But this is a small matter. The first contradiction—between success and love—turns out to be most important and prevalent in neurotic conflicts, as we will see later. Moreover, it is more directly related to the immediate causes of neurosis than the others. As Horney notes, all of us are subject to these cultural contradictions, but only some of us become neurotic.[24] Because the immediate causes of neurosis involve the quality of one's interpersonal relationships, the first contradiction between power (success) and love is most cogently related to interpersonal relationships. In Horney's view the principal cause of neurosis is the "lack of genuine warmth and affection" in early childhood.[25] The latter most often occurs as part of a parental ambivalence toward the child.

The basic anxiety underlying neurosis is "an insidiously increasing, all-pervading feeling of being lonely and helpless in a hostile world."[26] This basic anxiety is closely connected to a basic hostility toward others that the individual represses. The neurotic responds to a lack of love with hostility, but this hostility is unacceptable to admit to oneself and others; consequently it is repressed. Horney substitutes repressed hostility for Freud's repressed sexuality. Even if Horney is wrong at least in part about the basic cause of neurosis and about the idea of repression, her views on the basic anxiety, neurotic conflict, and cultural contradictions appear to be remarkably insightful.

Perhaps her greatest contribution is to describe how neurotics respond to the basic anxiety. In a sense it is the response to the anxiety that is the neurosis, or rather the response is an integral part of it. In short, the basic anxiety suggests that one's personal relationships are all problematic in that they invoke fear and hostility. The neurotic, then, possesses three ways of neutralizing the antagonism and potential harm of others: moving toward others, moving against others, and moving away from others.

Moving toward others often entails what she calls the neurotic need for affection. It may take the form of exaggerated dependence on others, a need to please, compulsive modesty, a need that everyone like me, oversensitivity to criticism, and so forth. The tacit attitude is, if people like me, they won't hurt me. Affection for others becomes a neurotic way of protecting oneself.

Moving against others involves a neurotic need for power and prestige often in the form of excessive ambition and competitiveness. Such people have to be right, have to win, and have to be admired. Every relationship is a competitive one in which there are only two outcomes—win or lose. The tacit attitude here is that if I am strong enough, no one can hurt me.

Moving away from people takes the form of emotional detachment from others, an excessive fear of commitment and responsibility to others, complete independence from others. The tacit attitude here is that no one can hurt me when there is no mutual involvement.[27] All three of these approaches to people are appropriate within limits. Dependence on and sensitivity to others is normal, as is some need for independence from others, and even at times the necessity to enter into conflict with others.[28] It is the compulsive nature of all three approaches to people that suggests anxiety.

These three ways of interacting with people are variously related to the basic anxiety: feeling lonely and helpless in a hostile world. With moving toward people there is a great emphasis on helplessness; moving against people centers attention on hostility; moving away from people gives priority to isolation and loneliness. In Horney's view, loneliness creates fear and fear brings forth hostility.

In her clinical experience, no one uses a single approach to anxiety exclusively. Neurotic conflict is the simultaneous use of more than one way of allaying anxiety. Indeed, all three—a compulsive going toward, going against, and going away from others—are present in the neurotic. The neurotic need for affection (going toward) and the neurotic need for power (going against) are most prevalent. Yet one of three modes of relating to others is always predominant. It is "determined both by the child's given temperament and by the contingencies of the environment."[29] Horney observes that for cultural reasons women tend to use the neurotic need for affection, whereas men more often employ the neurotic need for power as the predominant way of handling anxiety.[30] The other two modes, however, are invariably present, for the compulsive going toward, against, or away from others does not allay anxiety but increases it. Most importantly, the feeling of being lonely and helpless in a hostile world is a single feeling that simultaneously provokes a need to go toward, against, and away from others. Neurotic conflicts manifest themselves in a variety of forms: ruthless ambition versus a need to be liked by everyone; a need to avoid intimacy with others versus the need to possess and control someone entirely; compulsive need for independence versus pervasive feeling of dependency; attempting to remain in the background versus a secret desire to be a celebrity.[31]

In her later work, Horney began to realize that interpsychic conflict has its counterpart in intrapsychic conflict. Neurotic conflict does not just involve an approach to others; the conflict is also internal to self—between an idealized self and the real self (neurotic self). As she puts it, "Neurosis now became a disturbance in one's relation to self and to others."[32] The idealized self is a result of false pride that conceals self-hate. The neurotic hates his lonely, impotent, hostile self. This hatred of the real self involves a severe alienation from the self to permit the neurotic to live consciously in the world of his idealized self.

In effect, the idealized self becomes the cultural justification of the neurotic's predominant mode of relating to others in interpsychic conflict. The first "solution" to self-loathing is to create a self-effacing self that is, in the neurotic's eyes, unselfish, generous, humble, and loving. This idealized self corresponds to the neurotic need for affection present in interpsychic conflict. Therefore interpsychic and intrapsychic conflict are intimately joined at this point. Horney is quick to note that such an idealized self only occurs in cultures that place a high value on affection and dependency.

The second way of attempting to allay the anxiety of intrapsychic conflict is to form an expansive self, an idealized image that one is unique, masterful, successful—a great person. This idealized self corresponds to the neurotic need for power present in interpsychic neurotic conflict. This idealized self is only present in cultures that place great emphasis on individual success.

The third approach to intrapsychic conflict is resignation, to create an idealized self that one is independent, free, and self-sufficient. This idealized image is the counterpart to the neurotic going away from others. It magically transforms a weakness—emotional isolation—into a strength—independence and freedom. This idealized image too only occurs in cultures that place a high value on individual freedom.[33]

The neurotic is thus fighting a battle on two fronts—against others and within the self. From clinical experience, Horney came to realize that the idealized self was a major obstacle in getting the neurotic to admit his conflict and compulsive approaches to others that ensue from the basic anxiety he experiences.

The cultural values of love, success, and freedom form the cornerstone of the cultural contradictions Horney identified. Cultural contradictions do not automatically lead to neurosis, as indicated earlier. It takes the actions of others toward the neurotic, as well as the neurotic's own reaction, to produce the basic anxiety. By examining Horney's theory in relation to van den Berg's, we can begin to sort through the sociological causes—both cultural and interpersonal—of neurosis.

Van den Berg and Horney Compared

If van den Berg's analysis points to the most general sociological causes of neurosis, Horney's represents a study of an intensification of that sociological context. In short, Horney describes a greater ambivalence in one's relationship to others than does van den Berg. There are cultural reasons, I think, for this difference in emphasis. Van den Berg is writing about Europe, whereas Horney is studying America.

Both van den Berg and Horney regard neurosis as a disturbance in one's relationship to others and to self; both stress loneliness and fear as symptoms of neurosis. Horney places a much greater emphasis on hostility as a symptom of neurosis than does van den Berg. Van den Berg suggests that vague relationships to others result in multiple selves and the unconscious (unawareness). By contrast Horney centers attention on neurotic conflicts—simultaneous and compulsive movement toward, against, and away from others, on the one hand, and the conflict between a real and idealized self, on the other hand. In a sense Horney's discussion is more about the neurotic's response to the basic anxiety; it is about a second-order neurosis.

Van den Berg regards anomie and pluralism, ambiguity in the relations between groups and between individuals, as the principal sociological cause of neurosis. Horney thinks that cultural contradictions are the paramount factors in the form that neurotic conflicts assume and that they play an indirect part in the genesis of neurosis. Just as anomie and pluralism are differentially distributed in society, depending upon one's specific family, friends, and community, so too do the cultural contradictions differentially influence one's ambivalence toward others. In other words, groups and individuals do not exhibit these societal conditions to the same degree.

For Horney, the fear and hostility dimensions of the basic anxiety receive greater emphasis; for van den Berg, loneliness. Van den Berg stresses the conflict between multiple selves (social egos), whereas Horney calls attention to the conflict between the real and ideal self and the conflict in one's approach to others (interpsychic conflict). Both theorists (and therapists) are pointing to the disintegration of society. Van den Berg takes this anomic condition back to eighteenth-century Europe. Horney, it seems to me, is writing about the greater disintegration of society that occurs in a society, like America, with no cultural traditions to slow down and resist the ways in which capitalism and technology turn human relationships into competitive power relationships.

The cultural contradictions Horney discovered in the United States presuppose anomie (and pluralism); these contradictions, especially that between success and love, represent an intensification of it. Strong ambivalence toward others grows in an atmosphere of severe competitiveness and supplants the weaker ambivalence toward others that social ambiguity creates. Fear of and hostility toward others overtakes isolation and loneliness. Strong ambivalence leads to the interpsychic and intrapsychic conflict that is, as I have previously referred to it, a kind of second-order neurosis. It is a response to the extreme ambivalence that anxiety linked to hostility creates. In chapter 4 we will examine this ambivalence in greater detail.

Anomie and Contradiction in a Technological Civilization

Van den Berg and Horney take a holistic approach to the study of psychopathology. First, they realize that sociological factors are involved in the genesis of neurosis. As van den Berg puts it, all the various psychopathologies emanate from the same sociological context. Second, as van den Berg states and Horney implies, "A single patient, no matter to which group his illness belongs, embodies the entire psychopathology."[34] This is in sharp contrast to psychiatry and clinical psychology, which tend to take an atomistic approach of discrete mental illnesses with discrete causes. It will become apparent later that the individual patient contains the entire psychopathology, but now we must examine that larger sociological context that directly or indirectly foments psychopathology.

Horney wrote her first major book, *The Neurotic Personality of Our Time*, in 1937. She placed the cultural contradictions in American society into the context of capitalism, stressing competition, individual success, and advertising's stimulation of needs and desires.

Van den Berg's work came slightly later than Horney's, from the 1950s through the 1970s. His emphasis is on science as a secularizing influence in society. Our relationship to nature, society, and God becomes subject to scientific scrutiny and eventually is relegated to the private sphere. The result is anomie and pluralism in society. Concomitantly, van den Berg points to technology as a secondary factor in the disintegration of society. He appears to understand the idea of nonmaterial technology in his discussion of psychological tests and even professionalized psychology. What I wish to explore, then, is the role of technology (in the broadest sense of the term) as the sociological context for the genesis of neurosis and psychosis.

A technological civilization is a civilization dominated by technology. Here, I am following French historian and sociologist Jacques Ellul, who defines technology as "the totality of methods rationally arrived at and having absolute efficiency (for a given stage of development) in every field of human activity."[35] One of Ellul's critical insights is that technology takes in more than material technology (such as machines); it includes spiritual (nonmaterial) techniques, which are either organizational or psychological, or both. Bureaucracy is an example of the former, whereas advertising and public relations are examples of the latter.

Technology increasingly dominates every form of human activity. In the West, technological innovations were integrated into the extant culture until the nineteenth century; such innovations were situated in aesthetical, ethical, and religious relationships with other cultural artifacts and means of acting on nature. Historically, numerous limitations were placed on the use of technology, both within and between societies. First, technology was applied only in certain specific areas, such as production, hunting, and war. Second, the power of the technical means employed was limited in favor of the skill of the artisan and worker. The method was variable and adapted to the individual. Techniques continued to be used as long as they were effective; there was no insatiable desire for even greater efficiency. Therefore, technology was not readily discarded as it is today. Third, technology was local for the most part; it did not readily cross cultural boundaries. Fourth, there was a choice about whether to use technology or not. This is crucial. Because technology was so limited in its efficacy and because it was not the most important phenomenon in society, individuals were often free to choose among various methods, and to choose whether to use a technique at all. Today there is less choice. Today one pays a heavy price for not using technology, if only in terms of public opinion. Moreover, there is a strong tendency in a technological civilization to employ the single most efficient method when it is discovered.[36]

The upshot to this is that, prior to the nineteenth century, technology was simply one aspect of a culture and was without central importance. This began to change when scientific and technological advances, and the concomitant "myth of progress," swept across Europe and North America in the nineteenth century. Science and technology were inexorably linked; indeed, technology became the justification for science. The incredible efflorescence of technological inventions bedazzled leaders and followers alike; consequently, technology became an end in itself, the purpose of civilization. Ultimately, this desire to push technology as far as it will go has unintentionally led to technology's subjugation of culture. In other words, technology has become sacred.[37] Today, technology's total domination is exemplified in two societal processes: (1) in a technological civilization, everything tends to be an imitation of technology or a compensation for its effects[38] and (2) technology has become a system and our life milieu.

To appreciate the uniqueness of a technological civilization, we must con-sider technology as both milieu and system. A milieu is an environment, at once both material and symbolic, in relation to which humans face their most formidable problems and from which they derive the means of survival and some hope for the future. A milieu has three basic characteristics: im-mediacy, sustenance and peril, and mediation. We are in immediate and di-rect relationship with our milieu; it forces us to adapt, to conform, just as surely as we manipulate it. From the milieu we derive all that we need to live—sustenance for the body and the spirit: food, clothing, shelter, order, and meaning. Concurrently, however, the milieu presents the greatest threat to human existence, as in pestilence, famine, poisons, wild animals, political strife, war, and pollution. The milieu, then, is ambiguous in value and pro-duces an ambivalent reaction on our part—attraction and revulsion, desire and fear.

In Ellul's theory, humans have inhabited three milieus—nature, society, and technology.[39] Humans began the slow transition from the milieu of na-ture to the milieu of society nine to eleven thousand years ago, depending on the specific geographical location. The milieu of society arose with the emer-gence of the city, and the rise of civilizations and cities became complete five thousand to six thousand years ago. The movement to the milieu of tech-nology occurred in the nineteenth century and became more fully estab-lished with the widespread use of the computer in the twentieth century. El-lul's theory is no finalist theory in which the last stage represents the culmination of history; moreover, there is no deterministic principle under-lying the process.

Each subsequent milieu (for instance, society in relation to nature) medi-ates the preceding one, rendering it an indirect force. The preceding milieu becomes an ideological model for the subsequent milieu, thereby providing an illusion of where power resides. In dialectical fashion, however, it is actually the subsequent milieu that is used to interpret its predecessor. In the milieu of society, for example, nature is actually read through society, that is, it is an-thropomorphized. Therefore, nature as a model for society is, to a great extent, a nature that is already a reflection of society. Similarly, society serves as a model in the milieu of technology, but it is a society interpreted through a technological logic and thereby rendered increasingly technological. Each preceding milieu continues to exert an influence on the subsequent one, but the threat that it represents tends to become less important overall. In the mi-lieu of nature, the major problems were wild animals, poisons, and so forth; in the milieu of society the greatest threats are political and military conflicts; in the milieu of technology, the principal obstacles to survival are posed by technology itself, as with pollution and psychological stress. Not only does the subsequent milieu mediate the previous milieu, but it sometimes exacerbates the tensions and conflicts of the preceding one. For example, in the milieu of technology, political and economic problems are sometimes aggravated, as witnessed by increasing ethnic, racial, and nationalistic strife.

The most telling characteristic of technology as a milieu is that it actually (and not just theoretically) functions as a kind of open system.[40] Technology is an open system in that it interacts with its two environments—nature and human society—but it is not open in that it does not possess genuine feedback. What finally allows technology to become an open system is the widespread use of the computer. The computer allows each technique to become a source of information for the coordination of the various technologies. Technology is a system, then, at the level of information. This means, however, that each subsystem loses some of its flexibility, for its courses of action must be adjusted to the needs of the other subsystems. The mutual interaction and mutual dependency of subsystems made possible by the computer is the technological system. In large urban areas, for example, the various technological subsystems such as communication, transportation, law enforcement, and commerce become more dependent on one another for the smooth operation of the overall urban system.

Although the technological system is an open system, it is more or less autonomous (as a system) in relation to its human environment. The problem is that the technological system allows for no effective feedback, that is, self-regulation. Feedback means that a system (e.g., an ecological system) has the ability to correct the problem at its source. For instance, if the technological system possessed feedback, then the use of the automobile, a major cause of air pollution, would be eliminated or severely curtailed. Instead, we attempt to discover ways of countering the negative effects of the automobile on the environment. Only humans, however, can provide feedback for the technological system. But because of our supreme faith in technology and because of our delusion that as technology's creators we are its masters, we do not perceive the need to provide such feedback.

Even if we attempt to use the computer as a feedback mechanism, it can only handle quantitative data. Hence the computer rules out the possibility of evaluating the impact of technology on the qualitative side of life. Without genuine feedback, the technological system is out of control. This suggests a major contradiction—technology is simultaneously the paramount organizing and disorganizing force in society. Nowhere is this better illustrated than with what I described in chapter 1 as the suppression of subject and suppression of meaning.

The suppression of subject and meaning involves the objectification of the human through technique and the destruction of common meaning, an essential ingredient of morality. What both accomplish is to turn every human relationship into a relationship of power. The lack of a common morality or anomie makes relationships vague, dangerous, and competitive and thus present one with the dilemma of manipulate or be manipulated. Technique (or nonmaterial technology) promises one the ability to control others. Technique fills the void of morality, but it only reinforces the tendency for human relationships to be competitive. Hence it is not just capitalism, as Horney thought, that creates competition but also technology. Nor is it only the decline of a common morality with the rise of a scientific worldview, as van den Berg thought, but also technology. Science, which until the nineteenth century was independent from technology, eventually was joined to it and subordinated to it by the late nineteenth century.[41] Indeed, it is less science and more technology that provides our standard of truth: the ability to manipulate and create reality. This is a materialistic conception of truth—truth as power.[42]

The weak ambivalence that van den Berg discovered, ambiguous relationships born out of anomie, in a technological civilization becomes the strong ambivalence that human technique creates. Horney discovered strong ambivalence in the United States, a capitalistic society that is also the most advanced technologically.

Technology as both the supreme organizing and disorganizing force in society also means that the more rational society becomes, the more irrational actions and attitudes it manifests. Jacques Ellul observed that the more technically rational a society becomes, the more people need to escape into irrational pursuits that bring temporary amnesia or pleasure.[43] Humans cannot stand to have their lives fully rational, subject to timetables, lists, and rules. Their instincts require an outlet that produces an altered state of consciousness—mysticism or ecstasy.

In *Understanding Media*, Marshall McLuhan compared technology's psychological impact on the self to the physiological effect of injury or disease on the central nervous system. When faced with stress or irritation, the organism has two principal means of restoring equilibrium to the central nervous system. The first is the elimination of the irritant by overcoming it or escaping it; the second is counterirritation in which the central nervous system "amputates" (i.e., numbs) the affected limb or organ at the point of stress. Pleasure and therapy, McLuhan noted, are counterirritants, just as comfort is the elimination of stress or irritation.[44] Pleasure is a chief form of counterirritation. McLuhan's examples include alcohol, sports, and popular entertainment.

Apart from promoting the need to escape, technology enlarges the power of human instincts by liberating them from moral control. Every conventional morality places limitations on aggression, sexuality, and the like. In the milieu of society, the locus of a common morality is gradually split between the individual and the community. In societies that come to value the individual, reason, and freedom, self-control becomes a virtue.[45] The individual is expected to internalize a set of moral attitudes, not at times without some modicum of freedom in doing so, and to apply them even in the face of the opposition of others. When neither the community nor the individual controls the power of the instincts, they are given free rein; consequently, the impulse to satisfy one's irrational instincts grows more powerful.

There is a tendency for the individual today to equate the instinctual with the subjective. In a technological civilization reason is collectivized as technical reason; concurrently, subjective and normative reason, the ability to make judgments and to exercise critical reason, diminishes. The individual is rational largely in the context of technical and bureaucratic rationality, which in being centralized and collectivized requires little if any judgment on his part. Subjectivity comes tacitly to be identified with emotion. If much of my life has been colonized by technical and bureaucratic rules, at least my emotions are still mine.

The irrational finally becomes an ideal in that it represents the creative part of the self and an indirect resistance to the rational system that almost totally controls us. We tacitly sense that the more powerful the technological system becomes, the less powerful we are; that the more rational the system is, the less meaning and hope it can provide; and that our refuge is in the irrational.

Technology transforms shared meaning into instinctual power. Technology as an objective, logical procedure supplants human experience; the material visual image (technology's discourse) subordinates symbolic discourse to itself. The intersubjective based on human experience and expressed in discourse is replaced by the objective in the form of technology and visual images. Under these circumstances meaning becomes purely subjective and assumes the form of instinctual power and pleasure. Technology as the embodiment of instrumental rationality actually enlarges the domain and importance of the irrational (instinctual).

Widespread irrationality works to support the transformation of human relationships into relationships of power. Anomie unleashes the instinct to control and dominate others (the will to power), and technology makes a fundamental appeal to the will to power; for ultimately technology is about power. A growing irrationality fuels the basic anxiety and neurotic conflict.

In summary, there are at least four major contradictions produced by a technological civilization. The first is the contradiction between power and love. In Horney's formulation, the contradiction was between individual success and love. Love is still an ideological value, but technology even more than capitalism turns power into a value. Love implies a limitation on one's power over others, if not nonpower.[46] Chapter 4 on the neurotic need for love and for power examines how this contradiction affects neurotic conflict.

The second contradiction is between the rational and the irrational. As we have seen, the more rational (in a technical sense) society becomes, the more irrational it concurrently becomes. Chapter 5 on compulsive and impulsive disorders of neurotics analyzes this contradiction.

The third contradiction is that between power and meaning. At a certain level power destroys meaning. Technological power has led to the erosion of common moral meaning and created false meaning in its place. Chapter 6 examines how this contradiction plays itself out in the context of narcissism and depression.

The final contradiction is that of unity and fragmentation. Technology provides a rational unity for society; simultaneously it entails cultural and psychological fragmentation—multiple and conflicting selves. Chapter 7 describes how this contradiction is present in paranoia and schizophrenia.

The technological context with its various overlapping contradictions is the general source of all psychopathology today. The chapters ahead will attempt to demonstrate that each neurotic and psychotic embodies the entire psychopathology.

Notes

1. Karen Horney, *The Neurotic Personality of Our Time* (New York: Norton, 1937).

2. J. H. van den Berg, *The Changing Nature of Man*, trans. H. F. Croes (New York: Norton, 1961), 187.

3. J. H. van den Berg, *Divided Existence and Complex Society* (Pittsburgh: Duquesne University Press, 1974).

4. Stanley Diamond, "Schizophrenia and Civilization," in *In Search of the Primitive* (New Brunswick, N.J.: Transaction, 1974), 253–54.

5. Steven Lukes, *Emile Durkheim: His Life and Work* (New York: Harper & Row, 1972), 172–74.

6. Van den Berg, *Divided Existence*, chap. 6.

7. Van den Berg, *Divided Existence*, 131–32.

8. Van den Berg, *The Changing Nature of Man*, 164–69.

9. Daniel Boorstin, *The Americans: The Democratic Experience* (New York: Random House, 1973), chaps. 9–18.

10. Harry Stack Sullivan, *Conceptions of Modern Psychiatry* (New York: Norton, 1940).

11. Pitirim Sorokin, *Society, Culture, and Personality* (New York: Harper, 1947), 345–54.

12. Van den Berg, *Changing Nature*, 161–69.

13. Van den Berg, *Changing Nature*, 177.

14. J. H. van den Berg, "What Is Psychotherapy?" *Humanitas*, Winter 1971, 351–55.

15. Van den Berg, "What Is Psychotherapy?" 369.

16. Van den Berg, "What Is Psychotherapy?" 350–51.

17. Richard Stivers, *The Culture of Cynicism: American Morality in Decline* (Cambridge: Blackwell, 1994).

18. Van den Berg, "What Is Psychotherapy?" 358–70.

19. David Riesman, *The Lonely Crowd* (New Haven: Yale University Press, 1969), 81–82.

20. Van den Berg, "What Is Psychotherapy?" 364.

21. Van den Berg, *Changing Nature of Man*, 187.

22. Karen Horney, *New Ways in Psychoanalysis* (New York: Norton, 1939), 172–77.

23. Horney, *Neurotic Personality*, 288–90.

24. Horney, *Neurotic Personality*, 281.

25. Horney, *Neurotic Personality*, 80.

26. Horney, *Neurotic Personality*, 89.

27. Karen Horney, *Our Inner Conflicts* (New York: Norton, 1945), chaps. 2–5.

28. Horney, *Our Inner Conflicts*, 45.

29. Karen Horney, *Neurosis and Human Growth* (New York: Norton, 1950), 19.

30. Horney, *New Ways*, chap. 6.

31. Horney, *New Ways*, 215–17.

32. Horney, *New Ways*, 368.

33. Horney, *New Ways*, 176–78; Horney, *Neurosis*, chaps. 8–11.

34. J. H. van den Berg, *A Different Existence* (Pittsburgh: Duquesne University Press, 1972), 3.

35. Jacques Ellul, *The Technological Society*, trans. John Wilkinson (New York: Vintage, 1964), xxv.

36. Ellul, *Technological Society*, 73, 79–81.

37. Jacques Ellul, *The New Demons*, trans. C. Edward Hopkin (New York: Seabury, 1975).

38. Jacques Ellul, *Perspectives on Our Age*, ed. Willem Vanderburg; trans. Joachin Neugroschel (New York: Seabury, 1981), 48–49.

39. Jacques Ellul, *What I Believe*, trans. Geoffrey Bromiley (Grand Rapids, Mich.: Eerdmans, 1989), chaps. 8–11.

40. Jacques Ellul, *The Technological System*, trans. Joachim Neugroschel (New York: Continuum, 1980).

41. Ellul, *Technological Society*, chap. 5.

42. Owen Barfield, *Saving the Appearances* (New York: Harcourt, Brace & Jo-vanovich, 1957), 53–57.

43. Ellul, *Technological Society*, chap. 5.

44. Marshall McLuhan, *Understanding Media* (New York: McGraw-Hill, 1964), 42–45.

45. Jacques Ellul, *The Betrayal of the West*, trans. Matthew O'Connell (New York: Seabury, 1978), chap. 1.

46. Jacques Ellul, "The Power of Technique and the Ethics of Non-Power," in *The Myths of Information*, ed. Kathleen Woodward (Madison, Wis.: Coda, 1980), 242–47.

~

CHAPTER FOUR

Culture and the Neurotic Need for Affection and Power

In the following four chapters, we will examine a variety of psychopathological styles or forms, keeping in mind that they do not constitute discrete disorders or diseases. These are for the most part neurotic styles; the exception is schizophrenia, which is a psychosis or, more precisely, is psychosis. As van den Berg observes, psychopathology moves between neurosis and psychosis at the two poles.[1] These various styles reflect the contradictions of a technological civilization as outlined in the previous chapter. I do not pretend that my categorization of styles is exhaustive; instead, I mean it to be suggestive. Any forms not included in this discussion nevertheless emanate from this same sociological context. In this chapter we will examine how the cultural emphasis on power (success, winning, control) and the cultural emphasis on love (affection) developed and became intermixed. A consequence of this cultural contradiction is that neurosis quite often involves the conflict between the compulsive need for love and the compulsive need for power.

A Brief History of Love

In this section I will rely heavily on Beatrice Gottlieb's *The Family in the Western World* for a depiction of preindustrial family relationships in the West. Early in the Middle Ages, the paradox of an emphasis on celibacy and the inevitability of marriage was most pronounced. As the Apostle Paul taught, celibacy was a higher vocation, but it was not for everyone. It was better to be married than to struggle with lust as a single person. After the fifteenth century, the cultural emphasis on celibacy as a preferred state declined.[2] Still, only married persons were permitted to have sex.

Marriage involved other considerations besides sex; some of them were economic, others family-related. Especially in rural areas, marriage with children was a kind of social security, a hedge against the increasing dependency of old age. The institution of arranged marriage was a recognition that marriage affected the entire community. Nevertheless, arranged marriage was flexible in certain respects. Sometimes the potential spouse had the right of veto, if not the right to choose freely. The more wealth and political power entered into the arrangement, the more rigorous the demands. After the fifteenth century, there was a slow movement toward marriage based on romantic love among the middle and upper classes; the poor had been marrying for love all along, it appears.[3] Whether courtly or just romantic, love was a part of life, but sensible people were skeptical about it as the basis for marriage. Behind this suspicion was a recognition of the ephemeral nature of romantic love.

If romantic love creates a kind of equality, in marriage husbands and wives were not equal. The husband and father had more authority than the wife and mother, but their complementary relationships mitigated some of man's greater power and higher status. Because husband and wife were more or less autonomous in the performance of their complementary functions, they achieved a kind of partnership. Everyone believed that husbands and wives should come to love each other eventually, even if the marriage had been arranged. There is evidence, Gottlieb argues, of "affection, warmth, and devotion" in marriage throughout this period in all classes.[4]

Love had two meanings: sexual desire and the elevated spiritual state of romance. Recall that courtly love was sometimes conducted at a distance through letters and was not to be consummated if one of the lovers was already married. The Church worried about both kinds of love insofar as they were rivals to ethical and religious love.[5] Both sexual desire and romantic love increasingly were the motivation for marriage based on personal choice from the fifteenth century to the present.

The love of parent for child likewise underwent a major transformation during this period. Some historians, like Edward Shorter, have argued that prior to the nineteenth century parents did not particularly love their children.[6] In this view, modern child rearing is superior to that of the past. Other historians, like Gottlieb, provide us with a more complex picture of parent–child relations.

Prior to the eighteenth century, parents did not fully regard their children as individuals. Children had individual souls and thus were religious individuals, but they had no political rights and responsibilities and so were not political individuals. Because children existed for the sake of adults,[7] they were not full individuals even within their own families.

Children, who had many duties at a young age, were under the cultural authority of their parents. Peasant children could look forward to becoming servants with the obligation to their own family still intact. The cultural authority of parents depended on religious authority and the expectations of the community. Parents were the representatives of God, the Church, and the community. As such, they were obligated to discipline their children, that is, teach them to be unselfish and respectful members of the religious and secular community. Affection was a part of the larger process of discipline, not an end in itself. Gottlieb observes that in the past, child neglect was not about the lack of affection but about not exerting firm control of the child.[8]

Yet parents did grieve the loss of a child.[9] Strong feeling does not ensue exclusively from friendship or romantic love—aesthetical love (affection); it may result as well from common moral responsibility and shared obligation—ethical love. Parents did not need the affection of their children, nor were they overly affectionate. But they loved their children nonetheless.

Gottlieb argues that institutions have at least two emotional dimensions: (1) traditions and rituals in the institution evoke strong emotions and (2) the institution (in this instance the family) as a symbol stimulates an emotional response.[10] The institution of the family has undergone a radical transformation of its emotional significance since the Middle Ages. The most important changes have occurred in the past two centuries.

The nineteenth century witnessed a major change in the meaning of sentiment (see chapter 1). In the preceding century it was strongly associated with sincerity, a moral concept. The sincere person, who remained true to her moral convictions, was most capable of honest self-consciousness and of achieving a consistent, coherent self. In the nineteenth century the term "authenticity" begins to supplant sincerity. To act authentically means to act in accord with one's passions or emotions. Now self-consciousness depends on the strength of the emotions or energy that are expressed. Emotions are now autonomous rather than pressed into the service of a moral responsibility to others. Affection becomes an end in itself; love for a child is freed from the responsibility of guiding the child's moral development.

Humanists such as the eighteenth-century *philosophes* advocated the natural goodness of the child. Some Christians believed that baptism took away the child's sin. But innocence was short-lived, for everyone became a sinner once again on reaching the age of reason. Humanistic innocence was based on a view that the universal human as part of nature was good. Innocence was lost in a corrupt society, but fortunately society, and consequently childhood, was reformable. Affection for innocent children resulted in a fascination with them, even an expectation that the children would return the parents' affection.[11] Full-time motherhood, which increased rapidly among the middle classes, encouraged the idea that the intensification of affection between parent and child was the paramount function of child rearing.[12]

As Christendom took hold in Western Europe, the religious function of the family expanded. Parents had an obligation to God and Church to make sure their children remained Christian. The Reformation further strengthened the position of the family. The emotional significance of the family resided in members' common involvement in religious activities in and out of church. The modern saying that the family that prays together stays together indicates a major shift in attitude; it turns religion into a means for promoting family cohesion.[13] In the Middle Ages the inverse was true.

The emotional basis of the family has gradually moved from religion to internal family relationships. Family affection is now an end in itself, rather than a by-product of duties and activities that take one beyond the family. We will follow this story into nineteenth- and twentieth-century America.

Ann Douglas has described the use of sentimental love in nineteenth-century America. Sentimentalism in general conjures up feelings for the pleasure of the feeling; moreover, it traffics in nostalgia. In her view, sentimentalism asserts the values a society denies in its practices. Industrialized capitalism was making more and more relationships competitive and contractual. Sentimental love and family nostalgia were compensation for this.

Women and ministers became the advocates of emotion and affection because they were "chosen" by society to perform this function; it was now part of their identity and in the case of the latter professional identity. How did ministers and women become "feminized" (sentimentalized)?

Prior to capitalism and the emergence of middle-class Christianity, women had a complementary relationship to men, especially in marriage. There was a division of labor and relative autonomy in the performance of specific functions. Earlier the American wife had been self-employed in various home industries, had the right to vote, and was prepared to assume the husband's role as widow. By the nineteenth century, women's status and power had diminished with the emergence of the husband who had a monopoly on the economic function (women were increasingly full-time mothers) and exercised full control of domestic life. The wife-mother was compensated for her loss of status with the function of emotional sustenance.

The woman was valued not for herself, Douglas argues, but for the support she gave others, her ability to help her husband and children compete in a "heartless world." Her unselfishness and suffering were praised. In a short time, the American wife and mother was placed on a pedestal—she was a saint. This cult of motherhood eventually established the second Sunday in May as a national holiday—Mother's Day.[14]

Later in the nineteenth century women began to read and write "sentimental domestic" novels. One species of the novel concerned the grief parents experienced over their dead children. Reading the novel helped turn grief into a form of pleasure, "therapeutic self-indulgence." Those who mourned the death of a child in the novel were sometimes portrayed as "household saints" in the midst of an uncaring world. Other novels centered on the afterlife where heaven was a kind of home. In this spiritual home, one was reunited with dead relatives and friends. But for now home is as close to heaven as one can get.[15]

By the early twentieth century, government publications about child rearing for expectant mothers emphasized the "fun" mothers experience in relating to their young child.[16] Domestication can hardly go farther than this. The child becomes a toy or pet who exists for the sake of the mother. This represents in part a reversal—the self-sacrificing mother is now the mother who receives pleasure from her children.

Viviana Zelizer has traced the evolution of children from useful (in the early days of industrialization before child labor laws) to useless but highly valued. The child became a "sacred child" and was appreciated for his or her emotional value.[17] Besides bringing pleasure to the parents, the child allowed them to live vicariously through his accomplishments. The child became a projection of the parents' ideal conception of themselves.

The emotional value of the child indirectly points to what Douglas refers to as the second woman's role next to saint—consumer.[18] The latter role supersedes the former in the twentieth century. The woman had always purchased goods for others, but nonetheless this was her domain. As the shift from self-sacrifice for the child to self-projection through the child occurred, so did consumerism bring the mother more fully under its dominion. Now she could consume for herself, not just for others. The child had already been turned, at least in part, into an emotional commodity.

Feminization affected the minister as well as the woman. The strong seventeenth-century Protestant minister, both courageous and intellectual, gave way to the therapeutic minister who dispensed emotional support rather than theology and moral judgment. Religion, Douglas demonstrates, degenerated into "anti-intellectual sentimentalism." The minister lost his role as cultural leader at the same time his financial support from the congregation declined.

Consequently the minister looked to the secular culture for tips on how to keep his flock happy. The minister began to regard emotional "peace of mind" as his primary gift to the members of his congregation. The minister and the woman became both coworkers and competitors in dispensing affection.[19] Because the ministers were men, the feminization of ministers was the thin edge of the wedge. Eventually feminization would cut across sexual boundaries so that masculine self-control became a vice rather than a virtue.

The child as sacred object and source of affection for parents led to the idea that parents and children should be friends. As such they were equals with the same rights, goals, and even interests. As Tocqueville observed in the early nineteenth century, relationships in the family had become more equal as the authority of the father declined.[20] The emphasis was on cooperation, and parents came to believe that discipline would be acceptable to children if dispensed affectionately.[21] It was not a great distance to the belief that discipline and love were mutually exclusive. Parent and child eventually shared an interest in consumerism; the household became a private recreational center, with each bedroom a still more private rec center.[22]

An ideology centered on the phrase "haven in a heartless world"[23] featured a nostalgic view of the American family. The unity of and affection between husband and wife and between parents and children would sustain the middle-class businessman who faced ruthless competition each day. The purpose of the family was now therapeutic: each family member was the recipient and benefactor of affection as an end in itself.

A Brief History of Success in America

The seventeenth-century Puritans believed that America was to be the locus of a great religious experiment, an attempt to live out collectively God's kingdom on earth. Puritans, thwarted by the state religion of England, desired a situation in which the local religious community worked out the practical implications of being a Christian. Genuine freedom of the individual was nonexistent, however, as local churches exercised enormous control over the individual expression of faith.[24]

American Puritans eventually regarded economic success as one of the chief indicators of election to heaven.[25] As Richard Tawney notes, even though American Puritanism was the most totalitarian form of Calvinism, it too featured a theology that championed individualism. Nor did American Puritans immediately succumb to the seduction of an autonomous success ethic, for early on they were highly critical of those who took unwarranted profits.[26] Eventually the Puritan experimental community was transformed into a secular community in which individualism, especially economic individualism, flourished. By the late eighteenth century, Puritanism had lost most of its motivating force. "The victory of the bourgeoisie over Calvinism," Niebuhr proclaims, "was more total in America than it was in England."[27] With the triumph of a secular middle-class morality, economic success became a paramount cultural goal.

Benjamin Franklin was the first major proponent of a success ethic unencumbered by a Christian rationale. A deist in theory, he punctuated the first success manual with aphorisms: "Time is money"; "Credit is money"; "The good paymaster is lord of another man's purse"; "Remember, that money is of the prolific, generating nature."[28] His most important essays on the topic include "Advice to a Young Tradesman," "The Way to Wealth," and "Necessary Hints to Those That Would Be Rich." Weber regarded Franklin as the perfect embodiment of the spirit of capitalism. Yet even with Franklin the success ethic is not justified in hedonistic terms; instead, it is seen as the culmination of practicing natural virtues. Moreover, the purpose of individual success is to benefit the community. Like other Enlightenment thinkers, Franklin never equated self-interest with selfishness.[29] During much of the eighteenth century the yeoman farmer and independent property owner of middling income were the chief models of success.[30] It was not until the mid-nineteenth century that Americans openly defined success in economic, individualistic, and competitive terms.[31]

Books on achieving success are more numerous than those on any other subject in the nineteenth and early twentieth centuries.[32] This popular literature constitutes a wealth of information about American attitudes toward success. The novels, how-to books, pamphlets, and articles are not solely about success, however; happiness and health are also frequent themes. These materials form the heart of American popular culture during this period. They reveal how Americans who first associated success with moral character later linked it to the power of mind to motivate the self into a successful attitude (self-manipulation) and the power of personality to control both subordinates and superiors (manipulation of others). Success was eventually seen as a consequence of a psychological technique.

Even after success had been shorn of its peculiarly religious motivation, as with Benjamin Franklin, it retained a strong aura of traditional morality well into the nineteenth century: success and failure were viewed as a result of the presence or absence of character. By the 1830s the idea of success had been translated into a moral program. Achieving success requires the following qualities: industry, frugality, perserverance, initiative, sobriety, punctuality, courage, self-reliance, and honesty.[33] Success readily follows in the train of moral character; moreover, moral character can be inferred from success. So close was the identification of economic success with moral virtue that the two became as one. Moral virtue had become less important as an end in itself and more important as a means to economic success.

American ambivalence about success was expressed in the distinction between material success and true success. The former was represented as money, whereas the latter was defined in terms of individual happiness, the love and respect of others, doing one's best whatever the outcome, and peace of mind.[34] Most interesting for our purposes is the tendency to define true success as a psychological phenomenon even prior to the "mind cure" movement. Somehow the pursuit of true success was less offensive than single-minded devotion to material success. And yet turning happiness or peace of mind into an end in itself was just as antithetical to the spirit of Christianity.

The association of success with moral character is exemplified in the myth of the self-made man, who through sheer force of will and strength of character manages to rise from poverty to become rich and famous.[35] This basic plot line dominated both Christian and secular novels throughout most of the nineteenth century. There are many variations of the theme of upward social mobility. Rarely was the mobile individual truly poor to begin with; often he was of rural origin, confronting a hostile urban environment for the first time. The stories, while extolling success, were nevertheless directed against the perceived excesses of an industrial civilization. Hence the protagonist never devotes himself exclusively to the pursuit of wealth but rather upholds rural virtue. The hero never becomes a speculator (a form of gambling), rarely an industrial giant, but is usually an entrepreneur.[36]

The myth of the self-made man or "from rags to riches" is often associated with Horatio Alger, author of nearly a hundred novels for juvenile readers. He was the most widely read novelist of the self-made man. Writing in the late nineteenth century, Alger achieved his greatest sales in the Progressive period. Perhaps his writings, some have argued, compensated for the brutal competition of the Gilded Age. Alger's heroes are virtuous, gentle young people, not the acquisitive "fittest" of social Darwinism. Alger's writing provides idealized images of preindustrialized America, a time when the striving to get ahead was under control.[37]

Competing with the literature on success that stressed moral character was a serious literature that exposed the invidiously competitive side of the success ethic. The authors who wrote about success in a realistic way included, among others, Theodore Dreiser, Jack London, David Graham Phillips, Frank Norris, and Robert Herrick. They portrayed heroic, virtuous failures and unhappy, anxiety-ridden successes; they suggested that the children of the successful were often spoiled brats, and they implied that success was a specter that would not vanish even with reform. Criticisms notwithstanding, these realistic novelists had been socialized into the success ethic and finally came to see it as the foundation of American society.[38] Because they could propose no alternative, these writers embraced the very myth they criticized, something William James had observed when he stated that Americans exclusively worshiped the "bitch-goddess success."

Not all realistic descriptions of competition and success were critical, however. In the late nineteenth century, proponents of social Darwinism advocated unbridled competition and the "survival of the fittest." Applying Darwinian theory in ways Darwin himself would never have done, social Darwinists saw the successful businessman as the most fit member of the human race, as the one who had best adapted to the struggle for existence in the business world. Here there were no moral qualms about acquisition, for the belief in progress implied that morality went hand in hand with power. The fittest members of society (the strongest, the most successful) are the bearers of evolutionary progress, which extends even to the domain of morality. Hofstadter maintains that the British social Darwinist Herbert Spencer had some impact on the thinking of middle- and working-class Americans.[39] His theories were widely disseminated in popular magazines.

The main difference between the success-as-a-consequence-of-moral-character pamphleteers and the social Darwinists was not over middle-class morality. Herbert Spencer and William Graham Sumner were staunch advocates of the economic virtues. Rather, the difference lay in the ultimate justification for success: social Darwinists found the rationale for success in science and evolutionary progress, whereas the success manuals still turned to religion for an ideological defense. In the late nineteenth century, the uneasy truce between science and religion and the ascendant scientific worldview made it easier to pursue wealth—great wealth—without scruple. With evolutionary progress perceived as a deterministic process, power and goodness became identical. Success is not the result of moral character, nor even the proof that one possesses such character; rather it is moral character itself.

"Everyone knows that success with the great masses spells money," wrote John Van Dyke in his 1908 book *The Money God*.[40] By the 1970s success was most often defined as great wealth.[41] As we have previously seen, the Puritans defined success in less baldly materialistic terms; moreover, the idea of true success was often used to critique material success. These qualifications notwithstanding, the dominant idea of success from the seventeenth through the early twentieth centuries was that of individual economic success. In the late nineteenth century, however, two seemingly contradictory phenomena began to change the definition of success. Together they offered increasingly attractive alternatives to individual economic success. On the one hand, there is the rationalization and objectification of society in the forms of technology and bureaucracy; on the other hand, there is the extreme interiorization of human life so that everything not capable of being measured, of becoming a fact, becomes the merely subjective. Objective success became less individual and more collective, less economic and more technological; subjective success became a state of mind—happiness and health—and less a matter of production than of consumption.

In analyzing popular magazines, Theodore Greene discovered that by 1914 the new definition of success was "results" (efficacy), especially efficiency in the acquisition of results.[42] This, of course, reflects the growing importance of technology in the economy. The entrepreneurial function—the ability to revolutionize production "by exploiting an invention or an untried technological possibility for producing a new commodity"—was losing significance in the face of the routinization of technological progress, that is, the objectified work of teams of experts able to provide technical advice on every phase of the business operation.[43] Joseph Schumpeter summarizes this idea: "Rationalized and specialized office work will eventually blot out personality, the calculable result, the 'vision.'"[44]

The idea of technical efficiency leads to the idea of organizational efficiency, as evidenced by Taylorism. During the Progressive period organizational efficiency was considered the basis for reform, as well as upholding the traditional order. Labor and management, socialist and liberal, religious believer and secularist saw better organization as the key to economic and political order.[45] The success manuals, too, reflected this change.

At the same time that individual success was being transformed into technological and bureaucratic success, it was being translated into psychological success—happiness and health (well-being). Psychological well-being assumed two related forms: the consumption of goods and services to achieve the good life and the use of psychological techniques to achieve peace of mind.

As individual competition shifts production to consumption, success is redefined in terms of individual consumption. But consumption means self-increase, Elias Canetti reminds us.[46] The power of what is consumed becomes my power. Success is still about power even when it is defined as consumption.

Equality, Technology, and Power

Karen Horney pointed to capitalism as a source of competition and the foundation of the cultural emphasis on success (chapter 3). Although capitalism undoubtedly stimulates competition and a desire for economic success, it is not the only factor behind human relationships becoming largely if not exclusively relationships of power.

J. H. van den Berg argued that the norm of equality as an ideological response to anomie only furthered it. Anomie necessarily leads to individualism because it is not only the relationship between groups that becomes unstructured but also the individual's relationship to the group. This is why the modern ideology, as Louis Dumont calls it, emphasizes equality and individualism as opposed to hierarchy and holism in traditional ideology.[47] Hierarchy within holism means that the social structure is normatively integrated so that each group is related to every other group within the larger community. Consequently, relationships between groups and between individuals tend to be complementary and cooperative. Individualism and equality, by contrast, necessarily lead to competition. In a condition of anomie, competition becomes ceaseless and relentless because equality becomes exclusively an equality of power.

In contradistinction to this is the equality of love. If I love everyone as myself, I love each equally. I treat each person with equal respect and with equal regard to the other's well-being. Love is, in this sense, the way of non-power. Love suggests a normative equality, but an equality of power operates outside the normative dimension of culture.

Tzvetan Todorov suggests that Dostoevsky first understood anomic equality in the modern world.[48] Anomic equality leads to the master–slave relationship, a theme of Dostoevsky's *Notes from the Underground* that influenced Nietzsche's discussion of master–slave relationships. These relationships exist in a condition of "total competition." Equality in the context is transitory, for one quickly becomes either the winner (master) or the loser (slave). The master–slave relationship permits no third term—the equal. As Todorov notes, "the term 'equal' can only exist when it is negated."[49] To desire equality is evidence that one does not possess it. Yet becoming a master or winner is a hollow victory, for superiority is enjoyable "only on condition that it be exercised in respect to equals. If one truly believes the slave is inferior, superiority has no meaning."[50] Equality of power is a chimera in a condition of total competition. The anomic norm of equality creates total competition, which in turn destroys the limited equality of complementarity and cooperation.

Both capitalism and democracy foster competition that without normative control tends toward total competition. The third factor in turning human relationships into exclusive relationships of power is technology. Human techniques, like all technology, are about efficiency and control, or in other words, power. A child-rearing technique, for instance, is a logical sequence of steps that permits the parent to better control the child and to achieve the desired outcome—a docile high achiever. Human technique operates according to the principle of manipulation, whereas manners and morality function as normative reason. Manipulation leaves the other less free because it does not work rationally; human technique bypasses reason in its effort to control the other's instincts and emotions. Manners and morality typically placed restrictions on those with authority to enforce the norms; human technique, however, seeks to expand the power of the controller. The positive and negative reinforcement of manipulation, as behaviorists know quite well, works best the more power one has over another. Human technique is effective to the extent that all our relationships are subject to technique. Human technique fills the void anomie creates.[51]

Confusing Love with Power

Horney discusses the cultural contradiction of a concurrent emphasis on love and individual success as the context for the conflict between the neurotic need for affection and the neurotic need for power. The confusion today between love and power, however, both complicates and conceals the contradiction.

Before examining how the confusion between love and power manifests itself in marriage and parent–child relationships, let us examine two interrelated facts. The first, as observed by Horney, is that all relationships today have become competitive. This includes marriage, parent–child relations, and friendship.[52] The competitiveness of loving and passionate relationships must be concealed lest the ambivalence of the relationships become manifest. The second fact, according to Douglas, is that the growth of and pervasiveness of sentimentality, including sentimental love, is both compensation and cover for the competitiveness, anonymity, and unbridled power of modern life.[53] When love ceases to be a component of action, it can still exist as an independent feeling cultivated for its own sake, as with romantic love and the sentimental love of children. Sentimental love denies the power in the relationship between husband and wife and parent and child.

In a study of Columbia University college students, Herbert Hendin discovered that the relationship between men and women was marked by hostility, an unprecedented "pitch of anger between the sexes."[54] Men were concerned with hurting women, whereas women were worried about being harmed. Both men and women were attempting to avoid passionate feelings and moral commitment in their relationship with each other. Hendin gives a number of sociological reasons for this impaired relationship between the sexes, including the quality of family life, the overstimulation of our selfish instincts, cultural meaninglessness, intense competition, and the emphasis on the pursuit of trivial but exciting experiences.[55]

These same men and women eventually marry, swept away to varying degrees by romantic love. Many of these marriages eventually go under, as evidenced by the high rate of divorce in America. Michael Miller uses the term "intimate terrorism" to describe what happens among spouses who come to him for therapy. Intimate terrorism refers to a marriage in which each partner fears abandonment on the one hand and engulfment (being totally possessed) on the other hand. Such patients exhibit anxiety about each eventuality—to lose the other and to be owned by the other. The result is a marriage in which each spouse's actions are directed to one of the two unacceptable outcomes. The result is a concatenation of actions, each of which is a rejection of the other's perceived action of abandonment or engulfment.[56] Part of the reason for this romantic combat is the confusion between love and power. Someone who is too sentimental, he argues, loses a sense of the spouse's attempts at manipulation or subtle intimidation; someone who is too cynical about the spouse's actions becomes "paranoid and isolated."[57] The resultant confusion can lead one spouse to misinterpret the actions of the other. After romantic love begins to wane, sentimentality gives way to the tendency to manipulate the other without releasing the fear of abandonment. Intimate terrorism is an apt example of the neurotic need for affection (fear of abandonment) in conflict with the neurotic need for power (desire to possess, fear of possession).

Anomie necessarily entails the erosion of cultural authority. Tocqueville observed the waning cultural authority of parents, especially the father, in early nineteenth-century America, supplanted by public opinion and government. Were he writing today, he would enlarge his list of ersatz authorities to include the mass media (it was implied in his discussion of public opinion) and technical experts. Neil Postman and Valerie Polakow have argued, respectively, that the media and experts are robbing children of their childhood—their spontaneity, playfulness, resourcefulness, and creativity. According to Postman, the media accomplish this by enveloping children in an adult world so that the anxieties, desires, and experiences of the adult are vicariously consumed.[58] Polakow centers attention on the experts in the applied human sciences who manage and organize childhood so that it is merely an extension of adulthood.[59] Middle-class parents in particular depend on such experts for child-rearing advice. There is little of childhood that is not now an organized activity. One might conclude from such analysis that parents have a relatively easy time of disciplining their children. Perhaps this would be the case if it were not for the rampant puerilism of modern life.

Over sixty years ago, J. H. Huizinga called attention to the puerilism of modern society. In large part because many adult responsibilities at work and at home have been handed over to experts, the government, bureaucracy, and technology, we are imprisoned in a shallow adulthood. Moreover, anomie has weakened our moral responsibility to others in the community. Most characteristic of this puerilism is the inversion of work (and everything serious) and play.[60] We regard the serious activities of life as a game; business and politics come to be regarded cynically as a contest whose sole purpose is gaining personal advantage over others. Concurrently we treat sports, amusement, and entertainment with utmost seriousness. Witness the fanaticism of sports spectators and the amount of television coverage given to celebrities. Indeed television news has adopted the idea that it too must be amusing.[61] Huizinga mentioned the need for banal entertainment, the search for gross sensations, a propensity to be easily flattered, and an intolerance toward opinions other than one's own as further examples of puerilism. The upshot of this is that if children are too readily losing their childhood, the adulthood they are entering is puerile. Parents and children nevertheless remain in separate worlds because anomie and the specialization of work make the adult world invisible.[62] The media only provide the semblance of adulthood in their representations.

Without cultural authority the task of parenthood is difficult indeed. Permissiveness and authoritarianism are alternatives, but many parents choose, although not consciously, the option of affection as a form of control. Two studies have demonstrated its dynamics. Arnold Green made a comparative study of the male children of working-class Polish immigrants and the male children of college-educated middle-class parents in regard to neurosis. Ostensibly (or at least according to the psychological literature that stressed the lack of warmth and affection in early childhood as a leading cause of neurosis) one would have expected to find more neurosis among the Polish male children, for their parents rarely expressed verbal affection and often resorted to physical punishment. By contrast, the middle-class parents, especially the mother, often praised their children and showered them with verbal affection. Middle-class parents tended to rely on the advice of experts.

Middle-class male children, however, had a much higher rate of neurosis than their Polish counterparts. Green discovered that the very affection the middle-class parents display is indirectly behind the neurosis. "Personality absorption" is the term he provides for the "physical and emotional blanketing of the child" that creates an enormous dependence on the parents. The parents are overprotective of the child, and child pays a high price for it—the mother's threat to withdraw her affection. The dynamics are as follows: The parents (usually the mother) socialize the child to depend on a largely verbal love for his sense of self; then they use the threat of withdrawing it to control him. Constantly giving love and threatening to take it away act to produce neurosis.

Green asks, "Why love as a form of control?" The answer he gives is the romantic "love complex" in which love is seen as an end in itself and a solution to all problems. The parents "need" the child's love as much as the child "needs" the parents' love. But the parents also want to have children who compare favorably with the highest-achieving children. Parents compete with other parents as to who can have the best house, the best yard, and the best children. Parents live vicariously through the achievements of their children.[63]

In commenting on Green's analysis, van den Berg argues that the middle-class parents are displaying ambivalence toward their children.[64] They use affection and the threat of its withdrawal as a form of control, and they love their children best when they can "bask in the reflected glory" of their children. They need their children to display affection to them in return as a way of knowing they are good parents, and at times because of their own neurotic need for affection. Power and love are so tightly interwoven as to appear seamless. Overly dependent children are weak and in some ways more easily manageable. Such children often learn to manipulate their parents in return because they intuit the parents' need for their affection and accomplishments. Just like their parents, neurotic children may exhibit the conflicting tendencies of the need for affection and the need for power.

The confusion of power and love in marriage and the family highlights the cultural contradiction between success (power) and love that is represented in the most widespread neurotic conflict—that between the neurotic need for power and the neurotic need for love. Because personality absorption, overprotection, dependency, manipulation, and the need to be liked by everyone are widespread, and because they involve power masquerading as love, the neurotic need for power and love are difficult to differentiate and recognize. Moreover, not everyone exposed to a process such as personality absorption becomes neurotic; it has to be experienced in a persistent, intense way. Culture thus conceals the neurotic need for affection and the neurotic need for power.

The neurotic need for affection (going toward others) and the neurotic need for power (going against others) may be the most prevalent neurotic conflict, but it is not the exclusive one. The apparent solutions to the basic anxiety of being alone and helpless in a potentially hostile world involve going against, going toward, and going away from others. The going against others that is part of the neurotic need for power is easier to spot when it is not enmeshed with the going toward others of the neurotic need for affection.

The neurotic and psychotic forms discussed in the following three chapters are or have been recognized in the professional literature of psychiatry and clinical psychology and by the educated public. They are manifest, unlike the neurotic need for affection (and for power) that culture conceals, except in their most extreme expressions (e.g., radical dependency). The psychopathological forms in the chapters to follow feature moving against or moving away from others as the predominant way of dealing with neurotic conflict. The neurotic need for affection is not as well recognized because it is too threatening to realize that what modern culture calls love often takes the forms of an overly solicitous love, overdependency, and manipulative love. We console ourselves for the anonymity and rampant mistrust of modern life with the thought that love is alive and well. Consequently, moving against and moving away from others are more readily apparent in their psychopathological manifestations.

Notes

1. J. H. van den Berg, *A Different Existence* (Pittsburgh: Duquesne University Press, 1972), 110.

2. Beatrice Gottlieb, *The Family in the Western World* (New York: Oxford University Press, 1993), chap. 3.

3. Gottlieb, *Family*.

4. Gottlieb, *Family*, chap. 5.

5. Gottlieb, *Family*, 98.

6. Edward Shorter, *The Making of the Modern Family* (New York: Basic, 1975).

7. Gottlieb, *Family*, chap. 7.

8. Gottlieb, *Family*, chap. 8.

9. Gottlieb, *Family*, chap. 7.

10. Gottlieb, *Family*, 248–49.

11. Gottlieb, *Family*, chap. 7.

12. Gottlieb, *Family*, chap. 7.

13. Gottlieb, *Family*, 254–59.

14. Ann Douglas, *The Feminization of American Culture* (New York: Anchor, 1977), chap. 2.

15. Douglas, *Feminization*, chap. 6.

16. Martha Wolfenstein, "The Emergence of Fun Morality," *Journal of Social Issues* 7 (1951): 15–25.

17. Viviana Zelizer, *Pricing the Priceless Child* (New York: Basic, 1985).

18. Douglas, *Feminization*, chap. 2.

19. Douglas, *Feminization*, chap. 3.

20. Alexis de Tocqueville, *Democracy in America*, trans. George Lawrence (Garden City, N.J.: Anchor, 1969), 584–89.

21. Gottlieb, *Family*, chap. 8.

22. M. P. Baumgartner, *The Moral Order of the Suburb* (New York: Oxford University Press, 1988), chap. 3.

23. Christopher Lasch, *Haven in a Heartless World* (New York: Basic, 1977).

24. Richard Tawney, *Religion and the Rise of Capitalism* (New York: Harcourt, Brace & World, 1926), 72–91.

25. Kai Erikson, *Wayward Puritans* (New York: Wiley, 1966), 189–92.

26. Tawney, *Religion*, 112–15.

27. H. Richard Niebuhr, *The Social Sources of Denominationalism* (New York: New American Library, 1929), 104.

28. Benjamin Franklin, *The Works of Benjamin Franklin* (Boston: Hilliard, Gray, 1840), 2:87–89, 94–103.

29. Rex Burns, *Success in America* (Amherst: University of Massachusetts Press, 1976), 12.

30. Burns, *Success*, 1.

31. Burns, *Success*, 167.

32. Kenneth Lynn, *The Dream of Success* (Boston: Little, Brown, 1955), 3.

33. Richard Huber, *The American Idea of Success* (New York: McGraw-Hill, 1971), 95.

34. Huber, *American Idea*, 97.

35. See Irwin Wyllie, *The Self-Made Man in America* (New Brunswick, N.J.: Rutgers University Press, 1954); John Cawelti, *Apostles of the Self-Made Man* (Chicago: University of Chicago Press, 1965).

36. Richard Weiss, *The American Myth of Success* (New York: Basic, 1969), 35–60; Huber, *American Idea*, 42, 61.

37. Weiss, *American Myth*, 59–60.

38. Lynn, *Dream of Success*, 251.

39. Richard Hofstadter, *Social Darwinism in American Thought* (Boston: Beacon, 1966), chap. 2.

40. Quoted in Wyllie, *Self-Made Man*, 4.

41. Burns, *Success*, 167.

42. Theodore Greene, *America's Heroes* (New York: Oxford University Press, 1970), 319.

43. Joseph Schumpeter, *Capitalism, Socialism, and Democracy* (New York: Harper & Row, 1962), 132ff.

44. Schumpeter, *Capitalism*, 133.

45. Weiss, *American Myth*, 184–85.

46. Elias Canetti, *Crowds and Power*, trans. Carol Stewart (New York: Continuum, 1978), 353–54.

47. Louis Dumont, *From Mandeville to Marx* (Chicago: University of Chicago Press, 1977), chap. 1.

48. Tzvetan Todorov, "Notes from the Underground," in *Genres in Discourse*, trans. Catherine Porter (New York: Cambridge University Press, 1990), 72–92.

49. Todorov, "Notes from the Underground," 83.

50. Todorov, "Notes from the Underground," 83.

51. See Richard Stivers, *The Culture of Cynicism* (Cambridge: Blackwell, 1994), for a detailed discussion of this point.

52. Karen Horney, *The Neurotic Personality of Our Time* (New York: Norton, 1937), 284-85.

53. Douglas, *Feminization*, 3–13.

54. Herbert Hendin, *The Age of Sensation* (New York: Norton 1975), chap. 1.

55. Hendin, *Age of Sensation*, chaps. 13–14.

56. Michael Miller, *Intimate Terrorism* (New York: Norton, 1995), 28–32.

57. Miller, *Intimate Terrorism*, 24–25.

58. Neil Postman, *The Disappearance of Childhood* (New York: Laurel, 1982).

59. Valerie Polakow, *The Erosion of Childhood* (Chicago: University Of Chicago Press, 1982).

60. J. H. Huizinga, *In the Shadow of Tomorrow* (New York: Norton, 1936), 170–82.

61. Neil Postman, *Amusing Ourselves to Death* (New York: Viking, 1985), chap. 7.

62. J. H. van den Berg, *The Changing Nature of Man*, trans. H. F. Croes (New York: Norton, 1961), chap. 2.

63. Arnold Green, "The Middle Class Male Child and Neurosis," *American Sociological Review* 11 (1946): 31–41.

64. J. H. van den Berg, *Dubious Maternal Affection* (Pittsburgh: Duquesne University Press, 1972), chap. 6.

CHAPTER FIVE

~

Compulsive
and Impulsive Styles

Neurotic style, according to David Shapiro, is not a specific disorder but a mode of functioning that may be present in a number of so-called disorders. It includes behavior, ways of thinking and perceiving, and emotion.[1] In short, style is a way of relating to the world.

The obsessive-compulsive and the impulsive styles are well-known, even to the public. In the psychiatric and psychological literature obsessions, which involve thoughts and images, and compulsions, which entail actions (including mental), are rigid, ritualistic, and seemingly beyond one's control.[2] Impulsive thoughts and actions in general refer to the relative lack of intentionality and rational deliberation in actions that occur soon after the desire to act appears.[3]

Obsessive-Compulsive Symptoms

In the following discussion of the obsessive-compulsive and impulsive styles of neurosis, I rely heavily on Shapiro's analysis.[4] Few if any new symptoms are included in his study of these neurotic styles, but he offers a different interpretation of them. The obsessive-compulsive possesses rigid thought patterns and an unrealistic assessment of what is important. Three dimensions of the obsessive-compulsive style merit special attention—two involve thought, one action. The obsessive-compulsive person's actions often entail "tense deliberateness" and a feeling that he must precisely follow instructions and obey authority under all circumstances.

Obsessive-compulsive thought patterns are rigid in a number of ways. The obsessive-compulsive person is opinionated about many issues. This certainty comes from attention to detailed information. The obsessive-compulsive has an insatiable appetite for detail, but this narrow focus prevents her from entertaining different interpretations and questioning the facts. She appears to be concentrating with obvious effort, resulting in a loss of flexibility of attention and interest in a subject. The obsessive-compulsive is serious about every issue; everything is a problem waiting to be solved. The "normal person" by contrast possesses the ability to speculate on the meaning of facts and to vary the intensity and direction of intellectual interest. In short, the normal person is *flexible* in her intellectual orientation to a subject.

The obsessive-compulsive suffers from a loss of autonomy. Life centers on his work, not only his occupation but also his avocations: everything is transformed into work. The obsessive-compulsive seems driven and often chooses technical work that is repetitive and routine in nature. In all of his work, the obsessive-compulsive makes a continuous effort and appears to be "laboring over" each step of the task. But his effort is not so much with the task as it is with his effort. His attention is on himself. Shapiro uses the example of someone attempting to stop smoking to illustrate the difference between the normal person and the neurotic. The normal person focuses his will on smoking, whereas the neurotic's attention is on his attempt to stop smoking. The obsessive-compulsive is concerned with his will to stop smoking. In other words, does he really mean to stop smoking?

At the same time the obsessive-compulsive gives the appearance that all decisions are about willpower, she reveals the secret of her concern: her ability to decide and act is being strongly influenced (if not determined) by external factors. As Shapiro notes, the thought common to all obsessive-compulsive people is "I should."[5] The "should" actually emanates from the obsessive-compulsive person who acts as guard to herself as inmate. The obsession-compulsion issues commands, provides warnings, and admonishes the recalcitrant self.

Concomitantly, however, she perceives that the source of the directives is external. In a sense, she is the second in command who oversees her own inspection. The obsessive-compulsive person is aware that she is serving as a functionary in this regard but feels helpless to do otherwise. This self-awareness often takes the form of conscious role-playing (e.g., the obsessive-compulsive who performs the roles of wife and mother). The role-playing is so ritualistic that the role assumes the form of moral necessity. The obsessive-compulsive person sometimes experiences herself as an "automaton" who has an unlimited set of responsibilities and duties to perform. Shapiro recalls a compulsive patient who compared his life to a train "pulling a substantial load, but on a track laid out for it."[6] The sense of being directed by an external authority means that obsessive-compulsive people reduce their choices to technical ones—the one best way of doing something. For example, if such a person has to choose a movie to see, she might turn it into a problem of finding the cheapest, the closest, or most educational one.

Although obsessive-compulsive people spend an inordinate amount of time "researching" a problem, their final decisions are made abruptly. The reason for this paradox is that most decisions (e.g., choosing a movie) cannot be made in a purely technical way; there are aesthetical and ethical considerations that can never be measured and reduced to a logic.

Shapiro observes that obsessive-compulsive people suffer from a loss of a sense of reality, although in a special way. By focusing attention on the technical details of each action, they lose touch with the larger cultural context of life. Instead, life becomes a series of random actions for which one seeks a set of procedural rules. The normal person integrates details and technical considerations into a cultural interpretation borne out of and nourished by strong interpersonal relationships. The break with reality is not nearly as great as that of the schizophrenic, but nonetheless it leaves the obsessive-compulsive person with the experience of nihilism.

A sense of meaninglessness leads the obsessive-compulsive person to fluctuate wildly between dogma and doubt. He tends to be dogmatic in belief and ritualistic in behavior. The obsessive-compulsive person is highly susceptible to religious and political ideology, which invariably simplifies issues and provides him with absolute answers. At the same time, however, the obsessive-compulsive person suffers doubt about his beliefs when certain "facts" appear to contradict them. For example, a member of a religious cult may suffer doubt when the leader's predictions about the future are vague and later prove untrue. Shapiro attributes the interplay of dogma and doubt to a "technical mentality."[7] Dogma allows the obsessive-compulsive to resist new ideas, but the interest in technical details leads him to doubt his rigid and simplified beliefs.

The ritualistic, repetitive behavior of the obsessive-compulsive person makes her appear mechanical. It too is a feature of the technical mentality and of the perceived need to follow rules. A life that is fully subject to rules is completely ritualized. The major difference between neurotic ritualism and ritualism in traditional societies is that the latter is infused with cultural meaning. By contrast, the former is nihilistic.

In terms of Karen Horney's theory of how neurotics handle the basic anxiety—moving toward, moving against, and moving away from others—the obsessive-compulsive person has chosen the moving away from others as his predominant mode of protection from the basic anxiety. This is best illustrated by the flattened emotions that obsessive-compulsive people experience and express. Given that they are rigid and mechanical in thought and action, this is hardly surprising.

Impulsive Symptoms

The impulsive style of neurosis appears to be the opposite of the obsessive-compulsive style: impulse versus rationality. More than any other psychiatric or psychological category, the impulsive style does not fit any single diagnosis; it is present in a number of them.[8] The experience of an uncontrollable urge best characterizes the impulsive neurotic. Whereas the normal person experiences a certain intentionality in thought and a deliberateness in action, the impulsive person only senses an ephemeral wish that nonetheless feels irresistible. The perceived strength of the urge is often used as an excuse for the action (e.g., the keys were left in the open sports car) and an excuse not to change. This externalization of responsibility the impulsive person shares with the obsessive-compulsive.

The time between the urge and the action is brief; moreover, the action is unplanned. The normal person experiences urges and whims but is able to modify them or resist them. For example, she may purchase the least expensive whim or resist altogether the urge to purchase the Corvette. The impulsive person finds delayed gratification an unobtainable goal in large part because she does not have interests, values, and long-term goals beyond the satisfaction of immediate needs and desires. Her emotional involvement with others is shallow, and she shows little interest in politics, culture, and the life of the local community. Paradoxically, the impulsive person integrates her main impulses with a set of practical rules or techniques to realize them. For example, the underage alcoholic discovers ways to get adults to purchase the alcohol, bars where she doesn't need an identification, or places to obtain a false identification.

The impulsive person suffers from an inability to concentrate; this is related to his lack of planning. Moreover, he appears unable to think abstractly and to exercise good judgment and common sense. As Shapiro notes, the impulsive person's "initial impression . . . becomes . . . his final conclusion."[9] His cognition is passive in that he only reacts to urges but active in developing strategies to satisfy the urges. Tethered to short-term desires and frustrations, the impulsive person is characterized by reason that is fragmented and rendered subservient to his impulses.

Shapiro identifies two main variants of the impulsive disorder: psychopathic (active) and passive (weak) impulsivity.[10] The psychopath appears to be devoid of conscience and driven almost exclusively by the will to power. His utter insincerity includes a proclivity to lying. Some psychopaths can be quite charming and likable, but they share with all impulsive types a lack of deep emotion. Because the psychopath does so much harm to others, his form of impulsive neurosis involves the going against others as a principal way of handling the basic anxiety.

The passive or weak impulsive person is characterized by a sense of powerlessness, not merely in regard to his impulses but also in relation to others. In the latter sense, he is an extreme example of the other-directed character type. Rather than seek out temptation, the passive type is more willing to wait for the circumstances in which urge and group pressure come together before succumbing to the impulse to act. The passive type of impulsive lacks the capacity for friendship and love, and thus the moving away from others is his chief mode of attempting to resolve the basic anxiety. Weak impulsive persons sometimes become addicted to one thing or another: drugs, alcohol, shopping, and so forth. Much of the vast self-help movement is about recovery from various addictions.[11]

The Obsessive-Compulsive Style in the Context of a Technological Civilization

Like all forms of neurosis, the obsessive-compulsive style is an exaggeration and intensification of the sociological context: the obsessive-compulsive style reflects technological and bureaucratic rationality. As we have already seen, van den Berg pointed to the role of technology and science in creating multiple selves and the unconscious in the modern world. More recently Gerald Grumet related the obsessive-compulsive type to bureaucracy and technology, in particular their totalitarian aspects.[12] Much of what he describes, however, has been discussed in bits and pieces elsewhere.

Both Karl Marx and Max Weber referred to a phenomenon termed "the bureaucratic mind," recognizing not only that every organization produces a psychological mode of adaptation, a mind-set so to speak, but also, and more importantly, that the bureaucratic mind-set is a near total one. It is split between seemingly contradictory attitudes: "the deification of authority and consideration of the world as a mere object of bureaucratic action."[13] In a more general technological context, this mind-set views life *exclusively* in terms of adjustment to and manipulation of reality. When one makes reality (a purely material reality of objects and power relations) the ultimate

criterion for action, then there are only two possibilities: an ethic of manipulation (world as an object of bureaucratic action) or an ethic of adjustment
(deification of authority). Both are demanded simultaneously, however, and
both consist of technical rules. As C. Wright Mills observes, "To the bureau-
crat, the world is a world of facts to be treated in accordance with firm rules":
rules of manipulation and rules of adjustment.[14]

Stanley Milgram called attention to the phenomenon in *Obedience to Authority*. Originally Milgram wanted to investigate why so many Germans ac-
quiesced to the hideous Final Solution enacted by the Nazis. Turned down by
the German government, he conducted a series of experiments in New
Haven, Connecticut. His real purpose was to determine how far an individual (the teacher) would go in applying an electrical shock to another individual (the learner) who was purportedly attempting to learn a language or
some other body of knowledge. The teacher was led to believe that the experiment was about the effect of pain (punishment) on learning; he was unaware that the electrical shock inflicted on the learner who missed her questions was only simulated. Each time the learner missed a question, the
teacher was told to increase the "dosage" of the electrical shock that the
learner was only pretending to receive. The teachers in the experiment were
under no compulsion to inflict pain on the learners except for the orders to
do so. (The experiment had been designed so that the teacher could quit at
any time; moreover, the monetary inducement was rather minimal.)[15]

The results were startling: almost two-thirds of the subjects followed orders even to the point of giving to their learners what they thought could be
a fatal "dosage." As Milgram emphatically notes, however, the subjects were
not "monsters" but ordinary citizens from varied occupations and social
classes. At this point Milgram compares the results of his study to Hanna
Arendt's conclusion that Adolf Eichmann personified the banality of evil.[16]
Eichmann's defense that he was only following orders, that he was a mere
"cog in the machine," was not the defense of a diabolically evil person but
that of a normal person. As Arendt notes, this normality is "terrible and terrifying" because it signals that there are a large number of people who are unaware that they are doing anything wrong by simply following orders, no
matter what their content. More recently, Colonel Oliver North invoked the
same argument in the Iran-Contra affair. Milgram's results indicated that a
certain number of teachers experienced remorse about their actions when
they learned that although they had not inflicted pain on anyone, they had
been willing to risk killing someone in the name of science. The guilt that
some experienced was contradicted by the sociopathy of the obedience to authority syndrome.

One of Milgram's most incisive insights was that specialized technical tasks are incompatible with the broader view of context and consequences that moral decisions require.[17] To become fascinated with factual details or the details of the logic of a set of procedures is hypnotic in that it turns life into a game. A bureaucracy thrives on specialized tasks. Obedience to authority has become obedience to technical authority. No specialist can be the master of technical authority, the parts of which form a logical system. A moral agent takes the broader view; the technician never gets beyond his narrow specialization.

Bureaucratic organizations produce and make use of the obedience to authority response as well as conformity to the peer group. The distinction between obedience and conformity is often made on the basis of hierarchy versus equality. Authority is hierarchically structured, formal, and explicit; the peer group is based on equality (in principle), and its norms are informal and often implicit.[18] The modern organization collapses the social distance between the two.

Shoshana Zuboff has demonstrated that relying on information systems produces "anticipatory conformity." Information systems make work more visible; the computer contains traces of accountability. If the workplace is informated rather than automated, then the universal access to information creates maximum transparency: everyone's work is fully visible to others. If, on the other hand, managers retain control of information, then workers will either direct their anticipatory conformity toward their superior or alter the information they enter into the system to protect themselves. Information systems lead to the integration of production, thereby making workers more functionally interdependent; moreover, they reduce the psychological distance between the worker and the organization insofar as informated work requires continuous learning that, in turn, demands greater personal involvement than does automated work.[19] Consequently obedience to the manager is supplanted by the anticipation that one's peers will disapprove of shoddy work.[20]

Zuboff maintains that as organizations become more dependent on information systems, rationality replaces authority. In her words, "truth is the information system."[21] The implications seem plain enough: authority is vested in the information system; obedience to authority takes the form of obedience to information. Therefore, information systems concomitantly produce obedience to authority and anticipatory conformity. Bureaucratic authority is decentralized only to the extent that it is rationalized and centralized in the information system. The price is an ever greater blurring of the distinction between the individual and the organization.[22] Only individuals, however, are capable of acting as moral agents.

Obedience to authority is reinforced by psychological fragmentation: the development of multiple selves in which the individual becomes a mere role player. The reasons for this fragmentation include the rise of technology and the decline of common meaning. The implications of this for the obedience to authority syndrome are fairly obvious. The more one's self is fragmented, culturally and technologically, the less one is able to resist obeying technical rules—no matter how absurd, no matter how immoral. Only a unified self, a moral self, is capable of placing *specific* rules into a more *general* moral context. Man the role player is man the servo mechanism. The obsessive-compulsive person is the perfect embodiment of technological rationality.

The Impulsive Style in a Technological Civilization

Impulses are human instincts, which, not subject to individual reason, are irrational. Reason is associated with common sense, experience, and normative considerations on the one hand, and with scientific and technical rationality on the other hand. When the former types of reason recede in everyday life, the latter forms of reason, which are collective, generate ever increasing irrationality in thought and action.

To exercise common sense, learn by experience, reflect on that experience, and make moral judgments, the individual must be in immediate contact with reality. But technology causes us to lose contact with reality.[23] Technology makes our knowledge, opinions, and even emotions secondhand, for it mediates reality. In other words, it makes reality abstract. Technology at the level of means and knowledge must reduce reality to logical if not mathematical categories. But reality is sensuous, symbolic, and utterly ambiguous. To interpret reality I must bypass technology with a personal knowledge of history, culture, and other people. To the extent that I rely on technology, I reduce history, culture, and other people to logical categories and statistics. Public opinion, which depends on the mass media for its formation and dissemination, provides us with ready-made opinions on every issue. Moreover, the media, with their emphasis on visual images, manipulate our emotions about imaginary events and people. They provide us with vicarious experiences, thereby helping to release superficial and fleeting emotions. No one can remain rational in a subjective and normative sense if reality recedes into a series of random abstractions. If this happens, one will find reality in the irrational—instinct, emotion, and fantasy. The mass media, then, both mediate and compensate for an increasingly abstract reality with knowledge, opinion, and emotion that is only secondarily ours. Television in particular ensconces us in a shell of irrationality. The decline of common sense results in either an irrational use of reason or a retreat into the world of sensation pursued for its own sake.

Technology encourages us to lose touch with reality and makes us attempt to escape it as well. Technology increases the tempo of life: information is processed more quickly and human activity is more tightly compressed. Never before have people been expected to assimilate so much information and stuff as many activities into the day. This extends even into the realm of leisure, which is as technologically controlled as work. Humans often find themselves doing several things concurrently (e.g., fixing breakfast, listening to the news, and getting dressed). As Ellul observes, they are required to use reflex rather than reflection to respond to the fast tempo of life. The stimulus shield of a technological personality allows one to internalize some of the noise, information, and images that engulf us, especially if we have chosen such a lifestyle. But life is also subject to an endless list of regulations and schedules not of our own choosing. Under the tyranny of extensive rational control, humans feel the need to escape into fantasy, dreams, and ecstasy.[24]

Technology indirectly contributes to the tendency to escape reality by destroying the common meaning that is the foundation of every culture. As we have previously seen, humans do not perceive a need to symbolize technology (our milieu), for it is their own creation. Consequently, they do not create common meaning, which, among other things, attempts to limit the power of one's milieu. Moreover, the growing power of technology over the past two centuries militates against any attempt to develop a common morality. For there is an inverse relationship between power and values: when power becomes too great it destroys morality, which to be effective has to place some limitations on the exercise of power.

Apart from promoting the need to escape, technology enlarges the power of human instincts by liberating them from moral control. Every conventional morality places limitations on aggression, sexuality, and the like. In the milieu of society, the locus of a common morality is gradually split between the individual and the community. In societies that come to value the individual, reason, and freedom, self-control becomes a virtue.[25] The individual is expected to internalize a set of moral attitudes, not at times without some modicum of freedom in doing so, and to apply them even in the face of opposition from others. When neither the community nor the individual controls the power of the instincts, they are given free rein; consequently the impulse to satisfy one's irrational instincts grows more powerful.

Advertising plays on these irrational forces in order to strengthen them. The media in general provide ersatz norms in a context of moral meaninglessness. Visual images inform us about what is normal and what is possible.

But these norms, especially in advertising, assume the form of imperatives: "Buy this car; use this shampoo, you are worth it; run, don't walk, to our dealership; you must try this pasta sauce." These imperatives explicitly or implicitly say, "Don't wait." A speedy decision and immediate action are required. The impulsive person takes advertising to heart. A technological civilization does all that it can to make us act impulsively, rely on reflex, even as it subjects us to nearly total rational control.

A Dialectic of Obsessive-Compulsive and Impulsive Styles

We have seen that obsessive-compulsive and impulsive neurotic styles are opposites. Yet they emanate from the same sociological context—a technological civilization. There are striking similarities, however. In both types there is an absence of strong emotional involvement with others. The weak impulsive type and the obsessive-compulsive type likewise share a sense of powerlessness. Most telling, however, is the relative absence of common sense, moral judgment, and normative reason in the lives of both kinds of person. One leads one's life according to technical rules or impulse (instinct). Without moral restraint, technology is driven by the will to power. A technological civilization contains the contradiction of increasing rationality and irrationality.[26]

Herbert Hendin's study of Columbia University college students illustrates how widespread compulsive rationality and impulse are as ways of adapting to a technological milieu. Hendin describes how young men and women handled anxiety. Both sexes discovered two principal ways of avoiding strong emotional commitment to others: (1) a total "machine-like" control of one's emotions and (2) a giving-in to random sensations (the absence of control), such as drugs, alcohol, and sex. Although many individuals used both approaches, female students were more inclined to total control and male students to the absence of control.[27] Human relationships have apparently become so transitory, ambiguous, and combative that it is best to protect oneself against serious involvement in the life of the other. We sometimes have many superficial friendships as a hedge against the lack of genuine friendships.

The lives of protagonists in recent American fiction bear a striking resemblance to the lives of the college students at Columbia University. The underlying theme of this literature is that the most the individual with no shared sense of the past in a disintegrating culture can hope for is psychological survival, that is, for a "shock-resistant" life without passion. Josephine Hendin identifies two kinds of fiction that address this issue—holistic and anarchic.[28] In the former the characters seem to be attempting to achieve a "mechanical efficiency" in all activities, including their relations with others. A well-managed self becomes the way to survive in a world of ambiguous values and ambivalent relationships. Hendin points to John Barth as an example of an author of holistic fiction.

Anarchic fiction features characters in various stages of disintegration. Their lives are fragmented into a series of random mystical or ecstatic experiences. This response to the pain of serious commitment is in part a more passive response than self-management: one is enveloped in the pleasure of the moment. Kurt Vonnegut and Thomas Pynchon provide examples of anarchic fiction. The parallels between literature and life are remarkable here. The characters in holistic fiction closely resemble the students who choose the path of total control, just as those in anarchic fiction are similar to the students who give themselves over to the pursuit of random sensations.

In the following chapter, we will examine narcissism and depression. These neurotic styles reflect the contradiction of power and meaninglessness in a technological civilization.

Notes

1. David Shapiro, *Neurotic Styles* (New York: Basic, 1965), 1–4.

2. David Rosenhan and Martin Seligman, *Abnormal Psychology*; 3d ed. (New York: Norton, 1995), 266–67.

3. Shapiro, *Neurotic Styles*, 134.

4. Shapiro, *Neurotic Styles*, 23–53.

5. Shapiro, *Neurotic Styles*, 34.

6. Shapiro, *Neurotic Styles*, 40.

7. Shapiro, *Neurotic Styles*, 52.

8. Shapiro, *Neurotic Styles*, 134.

9. Shapiro, *Neurotic Styles*, 150.

10. Shapiro, *Neurotic Styles*, 157–175.

11. Wendy Kaminer, *I'm Dysfunctional, You're Dysfunctional* (Reading, Mass.: Addison-Wesley, 1992).

12. Gerald Grumet, "Tyranny of the Obsessional Character," *Psychological Reports* 68 (1991): 71–93.

13. Henry Jacoby, *The Bureaucratization of the World*, trans. Eveline Kanes (Berkeley: University of California Press, 1976), 154.

14. C. Wright Mills, *The Sociological Imagination* (New York: Oxford University Press, 1959), 117.

15. Stanley Milgram, *Obedience to Authority* (New York: Harper & Row, 1974), chap. 1.

16. Hanna Arendt, *Eichmann in Jerusalem* (New York: Viking, 1963), 253–56.

17. Milgram, *Obedience to Authority*, 7.

18. Ibid., 113–15.

19. Shoshana Zuboff, *In the Age of the Smart Machine* (New York: Basic, 1988), 296–97, 352–53, 401.

20. Zuboff, *Age of the Smart Machine*, 346–51.

21. Zuboff, *Age of the Smart Machine*, 356, 349.

22. Zuboff, *Age of the Smart Machine*, 403–5.

23. Arnold Gehlen, *Man in the Age of Technology*, trans. Patricia Lipscomb (New York: Columbia University Press, 1980), 78–81.

24. Jacques Ellul, *The Technological Society*, trans. John Wilkinson (New York: Vintage, 1964), 420–26.

25. Jacques Ellul, *The Betrayal of the West*, trans. Matthew O'Connell (New York: Seabury, 1978), chap. 1.

26. Richard Stivers, *Technology as Magic: The Triumph of the Irrational* (New York: Continuum, 1999).

27 Herbert Hendin, *The Age of Sensation* (New York: Norton, 1975).

28. Josephine Hendin, *Vulnerable People* (New York: Oxford University Press, 1978), chaps. 1, 10.

CHAPTER SIX

~

Narcissism and Depression

Narcissism and depression[1] appear to be "historically conditioned pathologies of the will," as opposed to pathologies of the mind,[2] and are emblematic of our time. One writer mentions that the "narcissistic ego" is dominant today, while another refers to depression as the "spirit of the age."[3] Some have even suggested a connection between the two disorders.[4]

Symptoms of Narcissism

The Diagnostic and Statistical Manual of Mental Disorders (4th ed.) refers to narcissism as "a pervasive pattern of grandiosity (in fantasy or behavior)" involving an excessive need for admiration coupled with an insensitivity to and a lack of empathy for others, usually beginning in adulthood.[5] Narcissism, according to David Levin, entails a "mask of omnipotence and aggression to conceal a profound sense of despair and helplessness."[6] Most obvious is the narcissist's feeling of superiority and of having the right to act and be treated accordingly.

The narcissist's grandiose sense of self-importance, fueled by fantasies of success, power, and popularity, lead him to exaggerate his abilities and accomplishments. His sense of uniqueness and importance border at times on feelings of omnipotence. Consequently, the narcissist not only demands excessive admiration from others but also has a sense of entitlement—that he should always receive special treatment, and that others should always comply with his requests (demands) and even anticipate his needs and wishes.

The narcissist is remote from others, showing little concern for their problems or empathy for them, and exploitative, making unreasonable demands on others but rarely reciprocating (e.g., the college student who uses his roommate as a tutor in math all semester long but refuses to assist the same roommate with her English assignments). The narcissist is often both arrogant toward and envious of others, disdaining their efforts and accomplishments. At the same time, however, the narcissist is overly sensitive to criticism and perceived slights.[7]

Narcissists often sustain a manic state of activity for long periods in part because of their perceived self-importance. Their "insatiable need for gratification"[8] is related to consumption in modern societies. As we will see later, consumption plays a central part in the creation of the modern self. We are what we consume. Joel Kovel calls narcissism a "neurosis of consumption."[9] The narcissistic self is all-consuming of goods, services, experiences, and others. The power of what is consumed becomes the power of the narcissist. When they experience frustration in their dealings with others and in obtaining what they want (and deserve), they sometimes express a childlike rage.

Narcissism as an expression of the neurotic will to power covers up profound feelings of powerlessness, helplessness, and inadequacy. The former compensates for the latter. The narcissist experiences powerlessness in conjunction with a sense that her life lacks meaning,[10] as do those who suffer from depression.

Karen Horney's concept of the neurotic need for power—the moving against others—as an attempt to allay anxiety approximates narcissism. In her later work, she observed that the neurotic person's relationship to his idealized self (see chapter 3) was as much a problem as his relationships with others. In her formulation, the idealized self was a consequence of false pride that concealed self-hate. The idealized self, moreover, mimicked the neurotic's predominant way of relating to others; for example, the neurotic need for affection is concealed beneath the idealized facade of humility, unselfishness, and generosity. Or again, the neurotic moving away from others becomes justified as the actions of a free person. The neurotic's idealized image resembles narcissistic grandiosity, even if some neurotic styles do not feature the neurotic need for power.

Symptoms of Depression

Depression is perhaps the best known form of neurosis; the media have made depression the poster child for mental illness. The depressed person appears dejected and is obviously brooding about something.[11] Internally she feels guilty about almost everything and experiences an almost "intolerable grief."[12] The latter is tantamount to mourning over one's dead self, a life that no longer has any possibilities and has become meaningless. This theme of meaningless is central to the experiences of the depressed person: there is no purpose or value to one's own life and to life in general. Everything is relative and in a state of flux. Everyday activities like eating and exercising hold little interest for the depressed person. Other people and beliefs have lost their ability to motivate the depressed person emotionally, although she may remain lucid about how her acquaintances and beliefs should be able to sustain her.

The experience of meaninglessness is intimately linked to the experience of hopelessness. The latter seals the tomb of meaninglessness and makes it appear eternal. Hope anticipates a future that is somehow and against all odds better than the present. The future may be related to a past from which it draws inspiration, but it is still new. Those who suffer from depression experience a serious distortion or even a denial of time. The present is stultifying and isolated from the future, which appears to be nonexistent, and from the past, which provides no consolation but only remorse.[13] The present has become a sort of hell that destroys both past and future.

The depressed person is passive and feels helpless, thus assuming the posture of fatalistic resignation. In severe depression, "paralysis of the will" is a common experience.[14] Concurrently, however, the depressed person is capable of going into a rage about a perceived affront.[15] Those suffering from depression are extremely critical of themselves and others; no one is spared their judgment. In a sense, everyone is responsible for the meaninglessness of their lives.

Narcissism in a Technological Civilization

Narcissism is principally about the will to power, especially when one feels powerless. A technological civilization is the perfect breeding ground for narcissism.[16] Modern technology is exclusively about power, about the most powerful means of acting.[17] In traditional societies, technology was subordinate to moral and religious considerations and limits; by contrast, we have permitted technology to dominate and erode culture. Technical power is about efficiency, maximum effectiveness with a minimum expenditure of time, money, and energy. Modern technology exhibits "absolute rationality," according to Friedrich Juenger, as opposed to both functional rationality and normative rationality.[18] The implication is that technical rationality may be at odds with what is morally, politically, or even economically best for a society. Our relationship to technology is irrational, however, because we un-wittingly regard it as sacred. As indicated earlier, what is perceived to be sa-cred is that which is felt to be most powerful. This blinds us to the negative aspects of modern technology.

The narcissist's fantasies of success and power are fueled by what I have termed "technological utopianism," the "religious" myth that justifies technol-ogy. This utopian narrative is straightforward. Science and especially technol-ogy are leading us to a utopia of maximum production and consumption. Tech-nology ensures our collective survival and success in allowing us more efficient control of life and providing solutions to all our problems. This promised land is likewise a world of total consumption, where people possess perfect health, beauty, and eternal youth. They are free to do whatever is pleasurable and thus experience complete happiness. The myth of technological utopianism is promulgated through the liturgy of advertising. This myth (in the strong sense of the term) is as much a myth as the ones created by archaic peoples.

The myth of technological utopianism is present in the structure or logic of advertising. Neil Postman has exposed this logic most admirably in his in-terpretation of a classic ad, "The Parable of the Ring around the Collar." The ad typically finds a married couple who normally get along well in a com-monplace setting, a restaurant; a waitress notices the husband's dirty shirt collar and calls attention to it. The husband is upset and the wife embar-rassed. The next scene shows the wife using the correct detergent that elim-inates the unseemly ring around the collar. Finally the couple returns to the restaurant enveloped in ecstatic rapture.[19]

In Postman's analysis there is a narrative in the ad that takes this form: problem, solution, ecstasy. The problem is the dirty collar along with the hus-band's anger over the social embarrassment; the solution is the advertised brand of detergent; ecstasy is the satisfied expression on the faces of the cou-ple in the aftermath of the solution.

I see two distinct but closely related logics at work in this single ad. All ads contain either one or the other and often both of these logics. These two logics illustrate perfectly the two dimensions of the myth of technological utopianism: the objective power of technique and its subjective impact on the consumer.

These logics are (1) problem to solution and (2) discontent to content. The problem-solution logic was dominant in advertising until the early twentieth century in a product-information format.[20] These earlier adver-tisements, still relying on the text, described how a product worked more ef-ficiently than its competitors or simply how effective it was. The ad was like a scientific demonstration.

After 1925 advertisers began to appeal directly to desire, viewing the consumer as an irrational as much as a rational being. The visual image became the dominant force in advertisements; the text became its adjunct. Visual images were better suited to demonstrate consumer satisfaction than product efficiency.[21] William Leiss has identified three advertising formats in addition to product information. The "product image format" provides the product with a number of symbolic qualities by placing it in a natural or human context; the product comes alive. The "personalized format" suggests that the product and its use make you more of a person—happy, admired, respected, and so forth. The "lifestyle format" associates the product with a collective style of life that includes friends, activities, and satisfaction. These three formats—product image, personalization, and lifestyle—stress the relationship between the product and people, that is, the satisfying use of the product against the mere utility of the product.[22] Yet all four formats, which compose a unity, continue to be used.

This brings us to the second logic: discontent to content. Sometimes the discontent is explicitly shown, as in the "ring around the collar" ad. The husband is angry and the wife is embarrassed; both are humiliated. Using the correct detergent produces emotional satisfaction if not ecstasy. Often, however, the discontent is only intimated. Gunnar Andren has called this phenomenon the "Hollywood set." This kind of advertisement presents an idealized world that contrasts with the real world of anxiety and discontent. This is the reason, he maintains, behind the many nostalgic representations of the past.[23]

The two logics, problem/solution and discontent/content, correspond to the two major story lines on the myth of technological utopianism. Techniques solve all our problems objectively (success) while simultaneously providing us with maximum subjective pleasure through consumption (happiness). Therefore each logic implies the other, whether made explicit or not in the advertisement. The overall myth unifies the two logics.

If the world of advertising is truly a mythological world, then it exists outside of the dialectic of truth and falsehood as understood in a scientific sense. On this level, true and false refer to whether something is factual or not. But the world advertising creates is not actual but only possible. Like all mythologized rituals, advertising can withstand the negative test of reality because there is always a next time: the possibility of perfection and total fulfillment in the newest commodity.

In the nineteenth century, success and happiness were distinct cultural values, but success was gradually bifurcated so that one branch merged with happiness. In the early twentieth century, success was being redefined in collective terms—the success of the organization; the individual was now a "team-player." Individual success was being transformed into technological and bureaucratic success just as it was being translated into psychological success—happiness and health (well-being). Psychological well-being assumed two related forms: the consumption of goods and services to achieve the good life and the use of psychological techniques to allay the anxiety modern societies produced.

The devotees of mind power, as early as the late nineteenth century, advocated "ease, relaxation, and comfort" over the ascetic virtues associated with the character ethic.[24] By the twentieth century, beginning in the Progressive period, a different set of values—health, leisure, fun—replaced the rat race (striving for success in the business world).[25] Advocates of positive thinking, such as Dale Carnegie and Norman Vincent Peale, touted inner peace and serenity more than material success.

One recent study of the success theme concludes that success in the twentieth century became individual self-fulfillment.[26] A 1972 survey of American businessmen by the American Management Association found that the largest number of respondents defined success as the achievement of goals. Achievement was defined variously as satisfaction with one's outward performance; satisfaction with one's life; and satisfaction with a goal achieved, a task accomplished, or a job well done. Note that success has become psychological satisfaction. When other definitions of success such as self-actualization, happiness, peace of mind, and enjoyment in doing or in being are added to that of satisfaction, it becomes evident that close to 70 percent of the respondents defined success in predominately psychological terms.[27]

In the 1940s Leo Lowenthal's content analysis of popular magazines concluded that American heroes, "idols of success," were more often than not entertainers. Earlier the hero was someone whose work was integral to industrial productivity; the new hero was one whose work was a leisure-time pursuit for everyone else—an entertainer.[28] Individual success moved from the arena of production to that of consumption, argued David Riesman, when the product most in demand became the personality and when morality as defined by the peer group became largely a matter of taste. The peer group, a "tutor in consumption," set fleeting standards about how and what to consume—music, clothes, automobiles, sex, and other people. Riesman observed that "people and friendships are viewed as the greatest of all consumables; the peer-group is itself a main object of consumption, its own main competition in taste."[29] Success became popularity attainable through the psychological manipulation of others or patterns of personal consumption. Advertising has played an enormous role in this, for it presents all of life as a vast spectacle of goods and services to be consumed. Once again, individual success appears to merge with happiness, a psychological state.

Individual economic success did not disappear as an American value, but the intensity of its motivation was weakening. Success was becoming, on the one hand, more collective—technological, bureaucratic, and political—and, on the other hand, more psychological—health and happiness to be realized in consumption. Outside of advertising, the department store was the greatest force in making consumption a way of life. Michael Miller's study of the Bon Marché Department Store in Paris is wonderfully illustrative. Founded in 1869, this great store became a behemoth of consumption in a short time. The building was enormous and its architecture histrionic; it had the appearance of a theater or even a temple.[30]

The department store in the United States never reached the grandeur of the Bon Marché; still it was grand enough to be referred to as a palace. Not an American invention, the department store nevertheless took deeper root in America than anywhere else. In keeping with the democratic sentiments of its customers, the American department store emphasized "show windows," large windows at ground level that were used to display merchandise. "'Window-shopping' was the name for a new and democratic popular pastime."[31]

The uniquely American contribution to consumption was the mail-order catalog, which proved a boon to the farmer and other rural dwellers. Montgomery Ward and Sears, Roebuck and Company were among the earliest and largest mail-order companies. Between the early 1880s and the early 1900s each company's circulation grew prodigiously, Sears's going from just over 300,000 in 1897 to over 3 million in 1907.[32] The mail-order catalog became known affectionately as the "farmer's bible." This secular bible promised a different kind of joy—the happiness of consumption. Boorstin describes its religious significance:

> It was not merely facetious to say that many farmers came to live more intimately with the good Big Book of Ward's or Sears, Roebuck than with the Good Book. The farmer kept his Bible in the frigid parlor, but as Edna Ferber remarked in *Fanny Herself* (1917), her novel of the mail-order business, the mail-order catalogue was kept in the cozy kitchen. That was where the farm family ate and where they really lived. For many such families the catalogue probably expressed their most vivid hopes for salvation.[33]

The treatment of consumption in the novel (from the early nineteenth century on) is a sure sign of the cultural significance of consumption. For illustrative purposes I have chosen three novelists who describe consumption and offer insights into its variegated meanings. Balzac could rightfully be called the chronicler of consumption. From a bourgeois background he repeatedly showed how desire unleashed competitive emulation and acquisition caused the downfall of otherwise decent people. He had a sensitive eye for the detail of consumption (as Henry James had an ear for the detail of conversation) by which individuals distanced themselves from or identified with others—"the way a cravat was tied, how shoes were polished, the type of cigar smoked."[34] Even more impressive was his understanding of the images and objects of consumption. In his novels the protagonists are invariably "looking at each other and looking in the mirror," becoming images, lifestyles reduced to projecting an image. As the characters consume the various objects of display and desire, they become the servants of the objects.[35]

The American counterpart to Balzac is Sinclair Lewis. Writing in the early twentieth century, Lewis produced his most detailed study of consumption in *Babbitt*. Each scene contains a virtual catalog of consumer goods and services from clothing and furniture to the automobile. Each object symbolized something about the inner or outer person and her social rank. Lewis understood, as Baudrillard later did, that the disparate objects of consumption formed a symbolic system.[36] His description of the automobile hierarchy is to the point:

> A family's motor car indicated its social rank as precisely as the grades of the peerage determined the rank of an English family—indeed, more precisely . . . There was no court to decide whether the second son of a Pierce Arrow limousine should go into dinner before the first son of a Buick roadster, but of their respective social importance there was no doubt.[37]

For Lewis, unlike Balzac, the tragedy of modern consumption is that both collective meaning and personal identity are inscribed in the objects of consumption.[38]

Don DeLillo, a contemporary American novelist, provides a humorous and incisive critique of consumption in *White Noise*. In a sense the main characters in the novel are television and the supermarket. DeLillo's insights into consumption are contained in this passage:

> Babette and the kids followed me into the elevator, into the shops set along the tiers, through the emporiums and department stores, puzzled but excited by my desire to buy. When I could not decide between two suits, they encouraged me to buy both. When I said I was hungry, they fed me pretzels, beer, souvlaki . . . They were my guides to endless well-being. People swarmed through the boutiques and gourmet shops. Organ music rose from the great court. We

smelled chocolate, popcorn, cologne; we smelled rugs and furs, hanging salamis and deathly vinyl. My family gloried in the event. I was one of them, shopping, at last . . . I began to grow in value and self-regard. I filled myself out, found new aspects of myself, located a person I'd forgotten existed.[39]

From the beginning of the eighteenth century consumption has been presented as the cornucopia of happiness. Astute observers, advertising agents, and novelists perceived that the relationship between the self and the object of consumption was becoming deeply symbolic and emotional. Initially consumer goods were sold as a means of achieving middle-class status. The principle at work here is social emulation. Upward mobility, in the ephemeral aspect of consumption, constantly shifting goods and styles, meant that one's status required frequent renewal. Set within the swirl of changing fads and fashions, the individual was at a loss to discern what the demands of status were; hence the consumer turned to the department store and the catalog for the most up-to-date models of status.

Because the "rhetoric" or form of display of consumable objects makes a fundamental appeal to desire, the act of consumption is an individual one. In discussing the implications of Lewis's novels about consumption, Neil Harris notes that the world of objects is not so much about obtaining status as forming an identity.[40] Colin Campbell ties the ethic of consumption to the Romantic definition of the self as infinite possibility: the unending search for new and intense experiences.[41] He concludes that "it would be just as true to say that the self is built through consumption as that consumption expresses the self."[42]

Yet it is just this distinction between status and lifestyle on the one hand and identity on the other hand that consumption blurs. In commenting on how the purchase of a Bon Marché tablecloth entailed the acquisition of bourgeois status, Miller explains that "images and material goods were coming to constitute life-style itself."[43] When lifestyle is reduced to consumption, the consumption of lifestyle becomes the consumption of consumption. This represents consumption taken to its logical and absurd conclusion.

There is an implicit pantheism in the rhetoric of consumption: I become what I consume; the powers of the objects of consumption become my powers. Two of the three symbolic advertising formats already discussed convey the idea of consumption as power. The product image format places the product into an environment—nature, society, technology—and thus gives it a certain determinism. The personalized format demonstrates how the product can transform your life, once again, power.

Because modern technology represents absolute rationality, we assume that it is subject to rational control. Actually it is driven by the will to power. For example, instead of living in harmony with nature, we attempt to subdue it. The relationship between modern technology and the human will to power is symbiotic.

A technological society is one whose chief value, purpose, or goal is efficiency, maximum production, and maximum consumption. Against rational technique stands inefficiency as instinct, the will to power. These opposite poles of a technological milieu, at a deeper level, are related. As Jacques Ellul notes, technology and instinctual desire form a dialectic: desire today can only be satisfied by technology, and technology can only advance by the constant stimulation of appetite.[44] Jean Brun first called attention to the paradox that the cold, impersonal, abstract force of technology does not finally appeal to reason and moderation but to our desire for power and possessions. Technology as a system is the "head of Apollo" superimposed on instinct— the will to power, the "body of Dionysius."[45]

The instincts most associated with the will to power are sexuality and aggression. As forms of inefficiency, sex and violence are the negative to the positive pole of efficiency (technology). If a milieu is composed of two poles in tension, and the principle of regeneration involves the movement from the negative to the positive pole, then the continuum between the poles is *excessive experimental consumption*.

The sacred power of technology becomes manifest in technological objects (consumer goods). These hierophanies of consumption become differentially sacred depending on individual circumstances. As already noted, technology, while manifestly opposed to instinct, is perfectly suited to it at a deeper level because both represent the will to power. Advertising uses sex and violence to sell these consumer goods (e.g., the eroticizing of the automobile). Even more importantly, the consumer goods of advertising are placed in spatial relationship to the sex- and violence-saturated programs of the mass media. In this sense programs are ads for advertisements. In consuming the technological object, we are indirectly consuming the instinctual power of sex and violence. Enlarge the sphere of the instinctual, and the desire to possess and use technological objects increases. The motto is: The more we consume (if only vicariously) sex and violence, the more technological objects we will consume; the more objects we consume, the more instinctual power we possess.

Narcissists experience powerlessness but fantasize about being omnipotent. A technological civilization reinforces these contradictory feelings by simultaneously making power abstract and reducing the power of the individual. Powerlessness takes the form of technological fatalism. Calling our faith in technology fatalistic may seem paradoxical, for modern technology is an expression of supreme confidence in our ability to direct the future. Traditional fatalism gave rise to a similar dualism of power and powerlessness. The differences between nature and technology, however, create a different dialectic in each case.

For traditional societies nature was the life milieu, the absolute value that served as a model of emulation. The power of humans was small against the immense power of nature. One's fate was tied to that of nature. The exercise of human power in the face of powerlessness assumed two major forms: the symbolization of nature and the attempt to discern the cycles of nature in advance. Symbolization brought nature under human control, if only as magic. Ritual was a way of appeasing and harnessing the forces of nature.

Technological fatalism is different from traditional fatalism in that it enlarges the scope and magnitude of human power. At first glance it should enhance our sense of power and diminish our sense of powerlessness. But for the most part it has just the opposite effect. Technology exacerbates our sense of powerlessness in two major ways. First, to the extent that technology becomes a system, power becomes objectified and abstract. Joseph Schumpeter observed that the nineteenth-century entrepreneur who knew every phase of his business gave way to the modern owner who depends on experts and consultants for knowledge he no longer possesses.[46] Moreover, as organizations tend to supplant institutions,[47] they become the technological context of our lives. Whatever technical power an individual might possess, he is nevertheless subordinated to organizational rules. Second, the more technology is applied to nature and society, the more life becomes unpredictable. The complex interactions of technology as they bear on nature and society create an ever larger number of unintended consequences. No mathematical model is sufficient to get all the variables; many of the most important can't be quantified. Furthermore, the use of systems analysis (as with information systems) actually militates against the flexibility required to deal with that which is unexpected.[48] We are thus double victims of our own logic.

This increased powerlessness to predict the future and solve the problems technology creates is not clearly recognized; our unlimited faith in technology clouds our perception. In traditional societies the negative outcomes never proved the ritual wrong (the ritual must have been incorrectly performed); in modern societies the negative outcomes never prove technology wrong. It only means that we need more and improved technology. No matter how irrational, our wager is on technological growth. At this point the prisonhouse of technological fatalism is sealed; we have no choice but to obey technological authority.

Depression in a Technological Civilization

Meaninglessness, time distortion, and hopelessness are essential symptoms of depression; a technological civilization produces the collective experience of meaninglessness and hopelessness while concurrently providing false meaning and false hope as compensation. Work, school, and leisure today appear to produce widespread feelings of boredom and even alienation. Studs Terkel's *Working* sheds light on the extent to which Americans find their work mortifying. In an interview shortly after the publication of the book, Terkel remarked that he was surprised to discover how widespread the alienation from work was; he said that he expected to find alienation among those with jobs that are repetitive and require little skill but not among skilled and professional laborers. Instead the alienation was omnipresent. In general the alienation assumed the form of a "lack of personal worth" in the work people perform.[49] For those who reveled in their work, Terkel mused that this may be more revealing about the person than the job.[50] Terkel, I surmise, is talking here about the ability of some individuals to rise above the lack of aesthetical pleasure in their work and find meaning in it. This suggests a limitation to a purely aesthetical view of labor, such as Marx's.

No matter how unpalatable the work may be, it can become meaningful when set in a moral context. Work that is an expression of reciprocal trust and respect in a moral community acquires an ethical meaning that transcends its aesthetical value. Without this, the work, no matter how satisfying, is meaningless. Perhaps the complaint against work today has less to do with its aesthetic value than with its bureaucratic and technological context, which militates against moral relationships between worker and coworker and between worker and client.

Students tend to experience school the way adults often experience work: as a necessary evil. Ralph Larkin's study of a suburban high school documents students' widespread estrangement from school.[51] The students are bored; this is the common denominator that cuts across all social divisions. Most students perceive the various ways in which they are being manipulated. When cultural authority declines, the only possibilities for control are coercion and manipulation.[52] The faculty do not fare much better in this bleak environment. Demoralized and apathetic teachers no longer perceive themselves as transmitters of a community's morality but as enforcers of bureaucratic rules.[53] In thinking that they are on safe ground with the latter, they unconsciously recognize that the bureaucratic rules are the effective morality of American society. The school has become an organization rather than an institution and as such is unable to persuade its participants—student and teacher alike—to believe in it.

More surprising perhaps than the boredom the students experience in school is the lack of joy they experience in sex and drugs. Experimentation with sex and drugs, as initiation rites into adulthood, appear to be compulsory—at least in the sense of having tried them. These activities, however, are entered into in the spirit of work rather than genuine leisure. Their compulsive pleasure is devoid of meaning and joy; it is almost as boring as the school they openly eschew.[54]

In a study of the English working class, a class Studs Terkel claims is quite similar to the American working class in aspiration, Jeremy Seabrook discovered that a higher level of consumption left people even more unhappy.[55] Consumption cannot offset the loss of tradition, the loss of function at work, and more competitive and violent human relationships. Technology, as we have seen, makes human relationships abstract and impersonal and destroys the efficacy of symbolically mediated experiences. This leads to an unhappiness that consumption and visual spectacle cannot overcome. And yet because technological utopianism promises us happiness, for us to admit we are not happy is tantamount to saying there is something wrong with us. Unless one challenges the myth, then the problem is with humans and their practices. We expect and are expected to be happy.

Boredom and unhappiness are universal, punctuating the lives of everyone from time to time. What is unusual is how widespread and constant boredom and unhappiness are today. Much of this can be attributed to the chronic meaninglessness of a technological civilization. The loss of common meaning is soporific; in contradictory fashion it produces a constant search for stimulation and new experiences superimposed on boredom. Modern technology destroys meaning, prevents new meaning from arising, and creates false meaning. Meaning here refers to ultimate meaning—the meaning of life, the meaning of history. All cultures are based on a sense of the sacred, an absolute value, which provides a meaningful unity. Absolute value is set in a narrative that offers an interpretation of the past (creation, our ancestors, etc.) and a way to achieve a perfected state in the future. Technology obviates the need for effective symbolic representations, for it promises us the good life here and now. Moreover, it destroys moral values.

There is an inverse relationship between power and values, Ellul notes.[56] Technology is first and foremost a powerful means of action. Modern technology raises power—political, economic, military, psychological—to an unprecedented level so that power itself becomes a value. But how does a growth in power lead to a decline in moral values? The answer revolves around the question of moral limits or boundaries. All moral values place some limits on the exercise of power. Freedom denounces the arbitrary exercise of power by a tyrant. Justice suggests that one is not allowed to take from another whatever one desires. Friendship prohibits the manipulation of one's neighbor. When power becomes too great, it is transformed into a value; moreover, it is a jealous value that permits no other. The discourse about moral values continues (as with the recent discussion of family values) and even increases, but the values cease to be effective values. They are reduced to a kind of ideological distraction that prevents us from seeing reality as it truly is. The human will to power appears to be stronger than the desire to limit that power, for the growth of power is intoxicating to any group or to any individual that may benefit from it. The growth of power, then, works to diminish (if not destroy) the effectiveness of morality.

Ellul identified three conditions that in conjunction make it virtually impossible for genuine meaning to be created: (1) human relationships become abstract; (2) human activity becomes trivial; and (3) action becomes ambiguous.[57] All three conditions are present today and are a consequence of the domination of technology. I have already discussed the first condition in the context of technology mediating human relationships. The second condition is a generalization of Marx's concept of alienation. To the extent that responsibility is centered in technology, bureaucracy, and government, my contribution becomes trivialized. If experts control my life, I become a passive consumer. The third condition has to do with the consequences of moral disintegration. When mutual moral obligation and trust weaken, our relationship to others becomes both vague and dangerous. We live in loneliness. The very conditions that cause moral disintegration make it difficult for meaning to be recreated.

At the same time, however, a technological civilization is a cornucopia of false meaning. What is false meaning? How do we distinguish between genuine meaning and false meaning? Genuine meaning springs from the lived experiences of people and flows outward so that it is embedded in the hierarchy of authority in that society; false meaning is external, imposed on people, and inconsistent with their lived experiences. Genuine meaning permits the integration of life's many activities, whereas false meaning is solely a compensation for certain activities that are harmful to cultural and psychological harmony.[58]

What kinds of false meaning does a technological civilization offer its citizens as compensation for this brutal treatment? Consumption in every form: goods, services, information, images, and personalities.

The health and happiness of the human body is the mythological goal of consumption. To consume means to increase. The power of the consumed object becomes my power. Advertising is an institution whose primary cultural function is to provide false meaning by turning every product into a symbol. Products are not merely useful—they must appear to satisfy deep ends, to mollify fears, and to create a new human being. For instance, the sports car symbolizes success; the cologne, sexual prowess; soft-drinks, fun and friendship. We consume false meanings every time we consume products and images in this civilization.

These meanings are false in a number of related ways. First, consumer goods and services cannot deliver on their symbolic promises: At most, the sports car brings you only the trappings of success; the cologne produces a minimal and temporary increase in attractiveness and cannot increase your sexual prowess.

Second, universal consumption leads to the reification (objectification) of the human being. My needs become objectified and fragmented in consumption. That is, each technological object or product is offered as a material solution to some human need. The number of products is virtually infinite; so too must be my needs. There is no sense here of a human whose needs are integrated, subjective, and finite but of a large warehouse of objectified and atomized needs and desires. The reified human is alienated from himself.

Third, universal consumption leads to the treatment of others as commodities—consumable objects. David Riesman observed that the consumption of other people's personalities has become an American preoccupation. To consume here means to treat the other's personality as an object that exists for my enjoyment and entertainment.

False meaning appears conspiratorial at its source, but is experienced as random in its consequences. False meaning is not the result of shared experiences that we make meaningful, but is inflicted on us in acts of manipulation that isolate us psychologically. The mass media reduce us to individual consumers of random information and spectators of random images. In turn the proliferation of such information and images makes life and human relationships appear random. Advertising, which is the chief dispenser of false meaning, is not guided by a conscious conspiracy to supplant genuine meaning with false meaning. Rather, it evolves as part of the technological system without decisive moral and political control. As genuine meaning declines, life is perceived, at least tacitly, to be like life in a Thomas Pynchon novel— both arbitrary and random.

Finally, Ellul notes that false meaning does not effectively compensate for meaninglessness but actually reinforces it; for false meaning is transitory and illusory.[59] False meaning constantly lets us down; our hopes are always being dashed. And the more meaninglessness deepens in us, the more we lose the will to resist and overcome it.

We vicariously live in the mass media, consuming objects that are superficially and ephemerally symbolic. The mass media objectify experiences and meaning (reified or false meaning). This contrasts with a traditional culture in which both experience and meaning are interpersonal: they arise out of everyday activity and a spontaneously created sense of shared purpose. The mass media as centralized agents impose experiences on us. Certainly we are willing accomplices, but this does not suggest that the psychological impact is a happy one.

Humans create meaning in their attempt to make sense of the tensions, conflicts, and problems of life. Most important perhaps are the issues of suffering and death. All traditional cultures had to face the question of the meaning of life in the face of daily suffering and imminent death. Compassion, friendship, and love were answers to the meaning of life, tragically conceived.[60] That is, life inevitably leads to death, and suffering rather than happiness is our daily fare; happiness is only an occasional respite from adversity. Technological utopianism contradicts the tragic view of life in substituting happiness as the permanent condition of human society and inadvertently makes compassion and love superfluous. For these acts only realize their potential in relation to human suffering. No wonder, then, that today we have "bereavement counselors" and can "rent" hospital visitors to offer encouragement to our loved ones.[61] It is best to ignore suffering and death as much as possible in our technological utopia; otherwise happiness may disappear.

Love, then, represents the possibility that adversity can both be given meaning and transcended. As Søren Kierkegaard observed, love is intimately tied to freedom.[62] Love is my freedom to overcome hatred, suffering, and even death. The freedom that love entails spawns hope. Without some modicum of freedom, hope is diminished. Love as a source of meaning intermingles with freedom as a prerequisite for hope. Hope is intimately related to meaning. In a sense, hopelessness is the experience that suffering is both meaningless and endless. Hopelessness, then, is an extension and intensification of meaninglessness. The despair of meaninglessness is in part a conscious despair; the despair of hopelessness is deeply unconscious.[63] With a partial awareness of despair, one retains the possibility of doing something about it; with hopelessness, one loses all will to resist. One begins to give in to the maelstrom of self-destruction.

Hopelessness is related to a distortion of time so that there is no future, only the present. For many, reality is on television or in the media, where everything is now, this moment, this instant. Existence has been typically experienced as a narrative—myth or history in the case of a society and biography in the case of an individual. Narrative contains two main characteristics: temporal succession and transformation.[64] Temporal succession can either be continuous—duration time—or discontinuous—event time. While narrative includes duration time, its paramount concern is event time. Events mark the significant occurrences in the life of a group or an individual; moreover, they take on a larger meaning in light of the story's denouement. Transformation refers to a critical change in the life of an individual or group. Reversal, as in conversion, is the paradigm of narrative change. Transformation, even more so than the event, has great symbolic power in a narrative; it has the ability to signify the entire story. Denouement brings together significant events and transformations in a way that makes the narrative a totality of meaning. In creating an "eternal present," television eliminates the historical context of events and places us exclusively in a random, incoherent present.[65] When we lack the ability to give meaning to suffering and the will to recall a symbolic past, including how our ancestors overcame adversity, fear becomes overwhelming. A "culture of fear" rests on a foundation of nihilism.

Despite the utopian promise of technology, it sentences us to a life of hard consumption, without meaning and without hope. Those who are capable of desacralizing technology can begin to search for meaning and hope elsewhere.

Dialectic of Narcissism and Depression

Both neurotic styles or disorders appear to be related to feelings of meaninglessness and powerlessness. The narcissist is active and aggressive (going against others), whereas, apart from occasional fits of rage, the depressed person is passive (going away from others). They have chosen different ways of reacting to the basic anxiety. Consumption confers mythological power and real meaninglessness. Narcissism is advertising's dream; depression, its nightmare.

The heavy incidence of both narcissism and depression is unusual. Narcissism is most related to the will to power, whereas depression is closely associated with powerlessness and meaninglessness. In the past, when societies experienced nihilism, it was less the result of a traumatic event (e.g., a crop failure) and more a consequence of a failure of religious or political authority. The disintegration of cultural meaning went hand in hand with the erosion of power.[66] Today power and existential nihilism coexist because technology at a certain threshold of power and influence destroys common meaning. In traditional societies, moral meaning was embedded in cultural authority. But technology is neither cultural nor human authority; rather, it is abstract and impersonal. A concentration of abstract power in the technological system and cultural meaninglessness are a chronic "dis-ease" of modern societies.

Of all the cultural contradictions identified earlier—power and love, rationality and irrationality, unity and fragmentation, power and meaning—the latter is the cornerstone of a technological civilization. From the conflict between power and meaning flow the other contradictions, implying that we are all mildly narcissistic and depressed today and that the neurotic forms of narcissism and depression are present in one way or another in all the other neurotic styles and even in psychosis (schizophrenia).

In the following chapter, we will examine paranoia and schizophrenia. These disorders represent the cultural contradiction of unity and fragmentation.

Notes

1. In this chapter, I drop the use of the term "neurotic style" and, following common usage, refer to narcissism and depression as if they were discrete disorders.

2. David Levin, introduction to *Pathologies of the Modern Self*, ed. David Levin (New York: New York University Press, 1987), 5.

3. On the "narcissistic ego," see David Levin, "Clinical Stories," in *Pathologies of the Modern Self*, 505. On the "spirit of the age," see the *Economist*, December 19, 1998, 113.

4. Levin, *Pathologies of the Modern Self*.

5. John Gunderson, Elsa Ronningstam, and Lauren Smith, "Narcissistic Personality Disorder," in *The DSM-IV Personality Disorders*, ed. W. J. Livesley (New York: Guilford, 1995), 205.

6. Levin, "Clinical Stories," 503.

7. Gunderson, Ronningstam, and Smith, "Narcissistic Personality Disorder," 205–6.

8. Levin, "Clinical Stories," 504.

9. Joel Kovel, *The Age of Desire* (New York: Pantheon, 1981), 106.

10. Levin, "Clinical Stories," 502–16.

11. Katherine Phillips et al., "Depressive Personality Disorder" in *The DSM-IV Personality Disorders*, 299.

12. David Karp, *Speaking of Sadness* (New York: Oxford University Press, 1996).

13. Levin, "Clinical Stories," 493.

14. Levin, "Clinical Stories," 497.

15. Levin, "Clinical Stories," 499.

16. Christopher Lasch explored the larger cultural context of narcissism over twenty years in *The Culture of Narcissism* (New York: Norton, 1978). The book resonated with the serious reading public and eventually became a best-seller.

17. Jacques Ellul, *The Technological Society*, trans. John Wilkinson (New York: Vintage, 1964).

18. Friedrich Juenger, *The Failure of Technology*, trans. Frederick Wilhelmsen (Chicago: Henry Regnery, 1956), 32.

19. Neil Postman, "The Parable of the Ring around the Collar," in *Conscientious Objections* (New York: Knopf, 1988), 66–71.

20. William Leiss, Stephen Kline, and Sut Jhally, *Social Communication in Advertising* (New York: Metheun, 1986), 189–90.

21. Leiss, Kline, and Jhally, *Social Communication*, 232.

22. Leiss, Kline, and Jhally, *Social Communication*, 231.

23. Gunnar Andren et al., *Rhetoric and Ideology in Advertising* (Stockholm: Liber Forlag, 1978), 152.

24. Richard Weiss, *The American Myth of Success* (New York: Basic, 1969), 15.

25. John Cawelti, *Apostles of the Self-Made Man* (Chicago: University of Chicago Press, 1965), 202.

26. Lawrence Chenoweth, *The American Dream of Success* (North Scituate, Mass.: Duxbury, 1974).

27. Dale Tarnowieski, *The Changing Success Ethic* (New York: American Management Associations, 1973), 43.

28. Leo Lowenthal, "The Triumph of Mass Idols," in *Literature and Mass Culture* (New Brunswick, N.J.: Transaction, 1984), 203–35.

29. David Riesman, *The Lonely Crowd* (New Haven: Yale University Press, 1969), 81.

30. Michael Miller, *The Bon Marché: Bourgeois Culture and the Department Store, 1869–1920* (Princeton: Princeton University Press, 1981), 167.

31. Daniel Boorstin, *The Americans: The Democratic Experience* (New York: Vintage, 1974), 104.

32. Boorstin, *The Americans*, 128.

33. Boorstin, *The Americans*, 129.

34. Rosalind Williams, *Dream Worlds* (Berkeley: University of California Press, 1982), 53.

35. Williams, *Dream Worlds*.

36. Neil Harris, "The Drama of Consumer Desire," in *Yankee Enterprise*, ed. Otto Mayr and Robert Post (Washington, D.C.: Smithsonian Institution Press, 1981), 209.

37. Cited in Harris, "Drama of Consumer Desire."

38. Harris, "Drama of Consumer Desire."

39. Don Delillo, *White Noise* (New York: Penguin, 1985), 83–84.

40. Harris, "Drama of Consumer Desire," 212.

41. Colin Campbell, "Romanticism and the Consumer Ethic," *Sociological Analysis* 44 (1983): 287.

42. Campbell, "Romanticism and the Consumer Ethic," 288.

43. Miller, *Bon Marché*, 184.

44. Jacques Ellul, *The New Demons*, trans. C. Edward Hopkin (New York: Seabury, 1975), 70–80.

45. Jacques Ellul, *The Betrayal of the West*, trans. Matthew O'Connell (New York: Seabury, 1978), 165–68.

46. Joseph Schumpeter, *Capitalism, Socialism, and Democracy* (New York: Harper & Row, 1962), 132ff.

47. Arnold Gehlen, *Man in the Age of Technology*, trans. Patricia Lipscomb (New York: Columbia University Press, 1980).

48. See Charles Perrow, *Normal Accidents* (New York: Basic, 1984).

49. Studs Terkel, *Working* (New York: Avon Books, 1975), xxix–xxx.

50. Terkel, *Working*, xiv.

51. Ralph Larkin, *Suburban Youth in Cultural Crisis* (New York: Oxford University Press, 1979).

52. Edgar Friedenberg, *The Vanishing Adolescent* (New York: Dell, 1959).

53. Larkin, *Suburban Youth in Cultural Crisis*, 150–51.

54. Larkin, *Suburban Youth in Cultural Crisis*, chap. 4.

55. Jeremy Seabrook, *What Went Wrong* (New York: Pantheon, 1979).

56. Ellul, *Betrayal of the West*.

57. Jacques Ellul, *The Ethics of Freedom*, trans. Geoffrey Bromiley (Grand Rapids, Mich.: Eerdmans, 1989), 463–65.

58. Edward Sapir, "Culture, Genuine and Spurious," in *Culture, Language, and Personality*, ed. David Mandelbaum (Berkeley: University of California Press, 1970), 78–119.

59. Ellul, *Ethics of Freedom*, 469.

60. Miguel de Unamuno, *The Tragic Sense of Life in Men and Nations*, trans. J. E. Flitch (New York: Dover, 1954).

61. John McKnight, "John Deere and the Bereavement Counselors," in *The Careless Society* (New York: Basic, 1995), 3–15.

62. Søren Kierkegaard, *Concluding Unscientific Postscript*, trans. Howard Hong and Edna Hong (Princeton: Princeton University Press, 1992).

63. Jacques Ellul, *Hope in Time of Abandonment*, trans. C. Edward Hopkin (New York: Seabury, 1973), 70.

64. Tzvetan Todorov, "The Two Principles of Narrative," in *Genres of Discourse*, trans. Catherine Porter (New York: Cambridge University Press, 1990), 27–38.

65. Neil Postman, *Amusing Ourselves to Death* (New York: Viking, 1985), 136–37.

66. Ellul, *Betrayal of the West*, chap. 1.

CHAPTER SEVEN

~

Paranoia and Schizophrenia

Paranoia and schizophrenia are in one important way polar opposites. The former is based on a unity of external opposition, whereas the latter is characterized by a series of fragmentations. Paranoia ranges from a mild neurosis to a variety of schizophrenia. In this section, we will consider the neurotic form of paranoia; later in the chapter, the schizophrenic version.

Symptoms of Paranoia

Paranoia manifests countless signs, especially its milder versions. Those who persistently hold grudges, do not forgive others, and take offense at every slight are at least mildly paranoid, as are those who are constantly jealous of others, doubting their loyalty and friendship.[1]

The most widespread characteristics of paranoia are suspiciousness and guardedness. The paranoid person is constantly preparing to deal with variegated threats, including insults, snubs, sarcasm, criticism, commands, or even physical threats. As David Shapiro notes, the goal of the paranoid is not to eliminate or avoid threats but to make oneself as invulnerable as possible to the threat.[2] And the best way to be prepared is to be suspicious of people, both their intentions and actions.

There are two main types in the paranoid style: (1) secretive, highly controlled, and passive and (2) arrogant, self-important, and aggressive. Both types share much in common but differ in their defensive posture. Type 1 conceals her suspicions as much as possible, whereas type 2 openly proclaims them.[3] The former is an example of the going away from others as the dominant form of resolving neurotic conflict; the latter illustrates the strategy of going against others. We will return to these types later in connection with paranoid defensive positions.

Paranoid people exhibit suspicious thinking that is above all rigid. They cannot be persuaded that their suspicions are unfounded, and they are highly selective in the way they marshal facts, perceptions, and innuendoes. In making the unshakable assumption that others pose a threat to them, paranoid people scrutinize every word and facial expression for signs of hostility, rejection, and even indifference. Like religious fanatics, they hold their perceptions and interpretations to be infallible. The paranoid are thus close-minded. Their inability to accept uncertainty and ambiguity further indicates paranoid rigidity: Better to anticipate the worst than to be surprised in a state of naive optimism. There is nothing more unsettling to paranoid persons than the unexpected, especially when it turns out to be unfavorable to their interests. Paranoid suspicion is a perfect example of self-fulfilling prophecy; in expecting rejection, they make it come true by rejecting their rejectors.[4]

Paranoid suspiciousness results in a significant loss of a sense of reality, although not as serious as that which the schizophrenic experiences. Because the paranoid person is convinced ahead of time of hostility directed against him, he ignores the obvious. He constructs a subjective world that participates in the larger intersubjective world of his culture only when it does not contradict his suspicious assumptions. He can find agreement with "normal" people about the facts, and if he is circumspect, he can keep his suspicions to himself. It is the selectivity and interpretation of the facts that sets him apart from others.

The paranoid person takes the facts out of context. Sociological context is interpersonal; the more one breaks with it, the more subjective is one's "world." This interpersonal context allows one to understand the words, gestures, and actions of others. Without this context, life becomes hopelessly ambiguous. Someone who wishes to protect himself against potentially dangerous people must be continuously suspicious of them. In a situation of near-complete ambiguity, suspicion is the best way to maintain security.[5]

Projection is an integral part of the dynamics of paranoia. Projection includes cognitive and affective aspects and revolves around the issue of autonomy. The central idea of projection is that internal tension, or motivation that one finds intolerable, is attributed to someone else. The content of the conflict or motivation need not be identical, however.[6] That is, my hatred of others does not have to assume the form of their hatred of me. For example, my anxiety about my competence may be projected onto my supervisor, whom I believe is unfairly critical of my performance and is looking for an opportunity to fire me. The transference of inner conflict to an external person or group is fueled by the rigidly suspicious interpretation of the actions of others.

Paranoia emanates from an intense threat to autonomy. Paranoid people live in a continuous state of vigilance and are ready for any surprise or emergency. Like an army, they can mobilize a number of defensive maneuvers: (1) an aggressive position of early attack, (2) strict self-control and exaggerated carefulness, (3) extreme vigilance.[7] Under perceived external siege, the paranoid exhibit "hyperintentionality" and consequently lose whatever spontaneity they once possessed. Every action and every word must be carefully planned. Spontaneity, including true sentiment and affection, is perceived as a sign of weakness; it marks one as a victim. The more rigid one's self-control the better; indeed, the tacit goal is to become an invulnerable machine. This probably explains the interest in machines that so many paranoid people have. Even before the act of projection, paranoid people possess an antagonistic relationship to the external world.[8]

The autonomy achieved by suspicion, hyperintentionality, and mechanical self-control is fragile, however. Actual autonomy, as opposed to the pseudo-autonomy of the paranoid person, is based on a sense of self-respect and feelings of competency. Self-respect is a broader idea than competency, for one can be less than proficient in an activity but still have integrity in the moral way one performs it. For example, you may be a businessman just making ends meet, but you still treat customers and coworkers honestly and respectfully. The paranoid person lacks both self-respect and a sense of competency.[9]

The paranoid's fear of external domination is matched by a fear of internal control.[10] If self-respect and competency provide a certain measure of freedom from instincts or the will to power, then their absence can lead to domination by the instincts. The individual who has realized her abilities has channeled her will to power in a creative way; in a sense she has "mastered" her instincts. The paranoid person fears his instincts, especially aggression.

The autonomy of the paranoid person is threatened on two fronts—internal and external. She becomes rigid on the internal front and defensive on the external one. Because the paranoid person has projected her internal conflict and sense of inadequacy onto an external force, any intensification of the internal problem produces greater suspicion and vigilance against the external threat. The external object of the projection represents an aggressive threat to the paranoid.[11] Internal and external threats are mutually reinforcing.

Earlier I mentioned that the content of paranoid projection is usually not a one-to-one match with the original motive or feeling of the paranoid person (e.g., internal hate projected to an external hater). The specific content of the projection is determined by the original internal tension or anxiety of the paranoid person and his defensive position, which includes both defensive concern (e.g., external criticism versus external coercion) and defensive orientation (e.g., furtive and passive versus openly aggressive).[12] The perceived hostility to the paranoid person is obliquely related to the original anxiety from which it springs.

The external threat provides a false unity for the paranoid personality. The paranoid process, Shapiro maintains, is "progressive and self-completing" so that a "disorganized and noxious tension" is transformed into a "tight, rigidly directed psychological system."[13] Those opposed to the paranoid person provide him with a negative unity, a conspiracy of common interest against him, and thereby give him a unity of defensiveness against his opposition.

Symptoms of Schizophrenia

J. H. van den Berg maintains that schizophrenia is simply another term for psychosis and that neurosis and schizophrenia are "the two opposite points in psychopathology."[14] Indeed, every symptom, every style, every disorder falls somewhere in between. Joel Kovel claims that it is not a specific disease but is rather a "collapse of being."[15] It is at the same time a serious break with a reality shared with others. Schizophrenia involves the loss of self (fragmentation of self) and the loss of a shared social world.

R. D. Laing identified three forms of schizophrenic anxiety: engulfment, implosion, and depersonalization. The fear of engulfment is the fear of being controlled by another's love or friendship. In this logic, love is a form of control that makes the loved one become more or less identical to the lover. Isolation from others is the only means of avoiding being absorbed by others. Implosion entails the fear that reality will obliterate one's identity. Although the schizophrenic paradoxically feels empty, the emptiness is his identity. Social reality—people, organizations, and institutions—will replace his negative identity with one of its choosing. The fear of engulfment and implosion contains the tacit assumption that social reality threatens to persecute him at every turn. The fear of depersonalization is fear of the freedom of others, who will invariably use their freedom to reduce him to an object. The potential objectification of his being requires constant affirmation of his subjectivity.[16] Every human relationship to the schizophrenic contains the seeds of his own destruction. More than anything else, the schizophrenic fears becoming a thing, a dead thing under the control of others. To protect a diminished empty self, he breaks with the world.

By all accounts, the schizophrenic lives a privatized existence. This isolation from others affects her sense of time and space. In effect, the schizophrenic lives outside time and space as if endlessly drifting in outer space. Psychologist Louis Sass mentions a patient who referred to himself as "a timeless being" and "the past as 'restricted, shriveled, dislocated.'" Another patient talked about the world as "an immense space without boundary, limitless, flat, a mineral lunar country."[17] Our sense of time and space is culturally defined, as countless studies have indicated. When someone is culturally dislocated in becoming completely isolated, time and space necessarily lose their meaning, definition, and limits.

Without a sense of time and space, the individual loses a sense of continuity, discreteness, and coherence. A unified self has the experience of being the same person over the course of a lifetime, of having a biography. This consistency of character allows one to become coherent to others. In chapter 3, we examined van den Berg's idea of multiple selves. Short of schizophrenia, the person still retains some, no matter how diminished, sense of unity. The schizophrenic loses even this. Sass cites one of his patients in this regard: "When I am melting I have no hands. . . . Why do I divide myself in different pieces? I feel that I am without poise, that my personality is melting and that my ego disappears and that I do not exist anymore."[18]

The loss of the self is perhaps best exemplified in the various fragmentations of the self. The basic split, according to Laing, is between the inner (true) self and the outer (false) self. The body is the core of the false self, but in general the false self is all that the schizophrenic hates about herself.[19] The body becomes merely one object among all the objects in the world, rather than an integral part of the self. In turn, the inner self becomes hyperconscious of the body or false self. The body becomes a foreign self and is continuously scrutinized. The inner self is a comment on and compensation for the false self.

In Laing's terms, the inner self becomes "unembodied" and strives to "transcend the world," including its foreign body.[20] The false self is despised and is nothing because, as we will see later, it is controlled by others. Paraphrasing Søren Kierkegaard, Laing asserts that the inner self is "all possibility"[21] and exists only in fantasy. At the same time, the body never reveals the inner self, which leads a secret existence. This rules out the opportunity for the spontaneous expression of genuine emotion. The schizophrenic's relationship to others is as distant as the inner self's relationship to the body. As we have seen previously, the love of others is perceived to be destructive; so too his own love of self. Consequently he "murders" his false self and becomes empty or nothing in order not to continue to inflict injury on himself.[22]

The false self is required to relate to other people, however. Since all human relationships are destructive, the false self attempts to minimize the intensity of the relationship to others. Nothing the false self does in any way brings happiness to the inner self; at best the false self can minimize the profound unhappiness the inner self experiences. The false self has at least three "strategies" to handle the threat that others pose. The first is to comply fully with the demands of others while pretending that one is an alien, a machine, or a dead person. As a result the schizophrenic's thoughts, feelings, and actions have no purpose. The second is that the false self increasingly assumes the major traits of the person to whom one has become subordinate. This can become a full impersonation of the person the inner self dreads and detests. Third, the false self assumes numerous transitory identifications with "small fragments" of the other's mannerisms and behavior. This becomes a kind of "compulsive mimicry."[23] The hatred of the other and the false self merge so that the hatred of the one being imitated and complied with is at the same time self-hatred.

Sass claims that hyperreflexivity is the "master theme" of schizophrenia.[24] Hyperreflexivity is an acute and persistent self-consciousness that encompasses an awareness of oneself and of how one seems to appear to others. For the schizophrenic, self-awareness is intensified and compulsive. Self-consciousness serves several purposes: (1) it keeps the false self under observation; (2) it assures the schizophrenic she exists; (3) it exposes her to danger because self consciousness appears to work in two directions—it provides knowledge to the inner self and the hated other who has merged with the false self.[25] In this instance, the other becomes a "persecuting observer."[26]

Schizophrenia is psychosis—a break with a shared reality and a retreat into a private world of fantasy about one's achievements and greatness. The inner self attempts to compensate for the hated false self but is frustrated because the false self is the only self capable of communicating to the external world. Therefore the false self becomes a kind of warden who imprisons the true self.[27] The inner self of the schizophrenic becomes more and more unreal over time, since it cannot be realized. It becomes impoverished and filled with hatred, fear, and envy of others.

The final step in the schizophrenic process is a splitting of the inner self. As Laing notes, one fragment of the inner self often maintains a sense of "I"; the other fragment then becomes "her" or "him." One of his patients proclaimed, "She's me, and I'm her all the time."[28] Now part of the inner self suffers persecution from another part. The world, the others, and the false self now include fragments of the inner self. In the most extreme cases of schizophrenia, almost everything becomes the enemy.[29]

The loss of self is intimately linked to the loss of the everyday world. Nearly total isolation is responsible for the shocking and seemingly inexplicable symptoms of schizophrenia: private language, delusions, and hallucinations. Kovel observes that discourse requires another person and a shared language.[30] In isolation from others, the schizophrenic creates a private language. Van den Berg draws a similar conclusion about delusions and hallucinations: they are a consequence of isolation. He discusses the amazing fact that most schizophrenic patients can readily distinguish between their perceptions and their hallucinations. Indeed, some patients give names to the "voices" they hear.[31] Perception is a shared world, as is conception. Unless catatonic, schizophrenic patients are capable of sharing perceptions with their therapists on occasion; they maintain a toehold in the world. Delusions too result from complete isolation. The more one is cut off from others, the more one's knowledge about others and the world in general becomes chaotic and arbitrary.

The concurrent loss of self and social world is behind the many contradictions of schizophrenia, including (1) solipsism and pantheism, (2) omnipotence and impotence, (3) omniscience and total ignorance, (4) meaningfulness and meaninglessness. The schizophrenic at times feels the whole world is in her or nothing exists but her; at other times that she has no self and is an object merging with other objects. The schizophrenic who claims to be omnipotent "will also say . . . that his body or his thoughts are under alien control." The same person will also be haunted by feelings of incompetence and ignorance.[32] The schizophrenic who is creator of all meaning declares the world to be meaningless.[33] These contradictions make perfect sense in terms of the inner self—false self dichotomy. In the private world of fantasy, the secret inner self of the schizophrenic is all-powerful and all-knowing—the creator of meaning. In the meaningless social world, the false self is impotent, ignorant, and without discreteness.

Paranoia in the Context of a Technological Civilization

How does a technological civilization contribute to the paranoid person's fear of external domination? The primary concern of the paranoid is autonomy. Much of what has already been said about modern technology answers this question, so I will be brief.

Autonomy involves the idea that my experiences, my knowledge, and my will play an important role in my beliefs, decisions, feelings, and actions. But technology objectifies experience. More of my decisions depend on the "advice" of technical experts. I become helpless in the presence of experts. However, even as technology makes me subservient to it as a user, it renders me powerless as a recipient. Those who exercise technical control in advertising, propaganda, and public relations, manipulate us psychologically. They provide us with secondhand emotions in the service of forced consumption. Technology's freedom is the superficial freedom of choosing between consumer goods, while the freedom not to be a consumer is denied.

Paranoid people often feel incompetent. At a certain level of power, technology deskills its users.[34] The more perfect the technology, the less perfect the human who employs it. Tools, for example, can help the artisan create a better piece of pottery; at a certain point, as with industrialized production, the machine does most of the work. The worker has become subordinate to the power embedded in the machine or tool. Computer software and expert systems make it less necessary for humans to think. Our knowledge is reduced to knowledge about the computer, not the world beyond it.

Technology makes power abstract in the process of objectifying knowledge and experience. Power becomes the power of the machine, the organization, the system. A critical aspect of the power of technology is its capacity for organization. Over a century ago, Max Weber understood that the power of bureaucracy is not in the hands of managers but in the system as a whole—in the coordination of specialized functions.[35] No one person could be knowledgeable about all aspects of the organization. Hence, those in power became subservient to the overall system of knowledge and rules. Weber's idea applies even more so to the technological system. As previously discussed, technology becomes a system when each technology is a source of information for the coordination of the various technologies. The power is in the system, not just a single technology.

Humans have trouble accepting the idea that power is not primarily in the hands of managers and politicians and fail to understand that power is abstract and resides in organization. Consequently, they look for conspiracies to explain undesired changes. If a single politician or businessman is not to blame, then there must be a conspiracy behind the recent downturn in the stock market, for example. The idea of paranoid conspiracy is widespread today, as evidenced in popular culture and literature.

In writing about the contemporary American novel, John Aldridge maintains that two frequent themes are "universal conspiracy" and "mass apocalypse."[36] Thomas Pynchon and Don DeLillo have dramatized both themes and the nexus between them in some of their novels. Universal conspiracy refers to the apparent interrelatedness of all human actions without the characters having the ability to understand and alter the situation. This leads, as Aldridge notes, to feelings of paranoia. The most improbable of events (e.g., an underground postal service in Pynchon's *The Crying of Lot 49*) appears to be related to other bizarre phenomena.[37] The reader, and usually one of the characters, has a sense of a "massive and mysterious" system that coordinates all human activity. At an emotional level, however, the characters seem to be falling apart; their lives exhibit maximum disorder. The reader is left with a sense that the human world at a sociological level is highly organized and at a psychological level highly disorganized. The simultaneous experience of order-disorder and the feeling that events are fully coordinated and yet beyond human intervention leads to a sense of apocalypse. I contend that the technological system is primarily responsible for such feelings of paranoid conspiracy. The technological system requires that each technology or subsystem be coordinated with other related subsystems. Never before in history have humans been subject to so many administrative and technical rules, which seem to proliferate without human intervention.

Anomie also encourages at least a mild form of paranoia. When human relationships become vague, they also become dangerous. One does not know what to expect of the other, who is now a potential competitor. We are all suspicious of one another today. Karen Horney once implied that in a highly competitive society, not to be suspicious of the other is more likely to be a sign of neurosis than the reverse.[38]

As already noted in the discussion of projection in paranoia, the onus of responsibility is placed on the paranoid person. The external threat is rooted in an unresolved internal conflict experienced by the paranoid person. Edwin Lemert's classic study of paranoia indicated that in virtually every case he examined, other people had conspired against the paranoid person. Not initially, but after months of hostility from the paranoid person, coworkers, for instance, conspired to get the paranoid person transferred or fired. Lemert concluded by suggesting that paranoid feelings of rejection and conspiracy have a certain validity. Paranoia may start out with projections, but the reaction of others may make the external threat a reality.[39] In a condition of anomie, friends, families, and coworkers are likely to retaliate and organize against aggressively neurotic people.

Schizophrenia in a Technological Civilization

In the earlier discussion of schizophrenia, several major themes emerged: fragmentation, depersonalization (engulfment and implosion are implied), and solipsism. A technological civilization encourages all three psychological tendencies in the mass media.

The impoverishment of the symbolic function of language is the foundation of the media's debilitating psychological impact. Symbolic thought, which is fundamental to the milieus of nature and society, employs the medium of language; technical thought, which is dominant in the milieu of technology, expresses itself in visual images, especially those of the mass media. Visual images are the language of technology.[40] Visual images in the company of atomistic words are meaningless, yet function as "symbols." They are in effect false symbols whose "meaning" is instinctual power. Technology symbolizes itself with these false symbols. Let us examine how this works.

Traditional symbolic meaning, like a metaphor, compares two words and that which they represent. In saying, "love is a rose," I create tension between the literal meaning of "love" and the literal meaning of "rose." The comparison is not to be taken literally but invites reflection. The meaning lies in the hiatus between the two words. The meaning in this example is quite complex and includes the ideas that love has to be nourished, that it can hurt (thorns), that it is beautiful, and that it blooms and fades. Often a metaphor involves comparing something less known and defined, *love*, with something better known and defined, *rose*.

Visual symbolism in the media does not exclude discourse and atomistic words, but incorporates and transforms them. For example, a famous Coca-Cola ad shows children of various cultures around the world holding hands and singing a song about friendship, "I'd like to teach the world to sing," and pictures of people drinking Coca-Cola. The symbolism involves key words and phrases, such as "peace" and "harmony," and two sets of visual images: children holding hands and Coca-Cola. Peace or harmony is associated with hand holding and both of these with Coca-Cola. This material symbolism reifies the atomistic and more or less meaningless words "peace" and "harmony" so that handholding equals Coca-Cola. The symbolism moves from less well known to better known in the following direction: from *peace* and *harmony* to children holding hands to Coca-Cola. The meaning of peace and harmony resides in Coca-Cola, a product that has the power to give me pleasure (first-order importance) and the power to create world peace (second-order importance).

This visual symbolism, unlike the metaphor, creates no meaning, for it is created out of literal or material associations. That is, *peace* and *harmony* equal holding hands, and holding hands equals Coca-Cola. Life consists of material relationships to people and to products. But the "meaning" of life resides in that which is powerful—technological objects like Coca-Cola. This is how technology symbolizes itself; we are its unwitting agents despite being its creators.

Only a symbolic universe gives us the experience of living in a concrete reality.[41] When language becomes too abstract, we are cut off from empirical reality and inhabit a world of personified abstractions. When language loses meaning, we live in a completely material world of instinct, sensations, and power—a frightening world of raw power, in which we must be suspicious and distrustful of others. It is a world that always appears on the verge of apocalypse.[42] Symbolic language allows us to experience and create a world that possesses ethical meaning and thus appears to be consistent, coherent, and worthy of trust. Concrete reality is a unified reality; only a symbolic universe can provide us with experiences that unite the abstract and the material.

Without effective symbolism, concrete reality becomes fragmented. Part of reality is lived in the dramatized information of the mass media, and the other part of reality is experienced in the statistical information housed in the computer. Reality is on television and in the computer. Before looking at television in greater detail, let us make a detour through the fragmentation and depersonalization of modern totalitarianism.

Tzvetan Todorov's masterful *Facing the Extreme: Moral Life in Concentration Camps* discusses the fragmentation and depersonalization of the individual in the context of totalitarianism, of which concentration camps are the fullest expression. The state assumes control of all social goals and appropriates the individual's social existence. In effect, the individual is denied moral responsibility for her actions. Fragmentation and depersonalization make it difficult, if not impossible, for the individual to exercise moral judgment. Fragmentation and depersonalization, then, represent the internalization of totalitarianism. These twin psychological maladies occur today in less extreme contexts.[43]

In fragmentation the self is split in a variety of ways, including discontinuity between the public and private spheres of life and between thought and action. Todorov provides the example of a Nazi guard who treats inmates in cruel ways at work but hours later is a kind and loving father to his children in the privacy of his house, and the inmate who retains his religious beliefs but informs on fellow inmates.

Manifestations of fragmentation in the modern world include technical and bureaucratic specialization and professionalization. Personal responsibility is narrowly limited to one's specialized function. No one person is responsible for a decision in the modern bureaucracy. Our responsibility is further diminished by our dependence on specialized experts, who have invaded all spheres of life.[44]

The more technology objectifies human ability and intelligence, the less one needs to rely on personal experience and tradition. It is easy to forget that technology affects us as we create and use it. What it requires of us in an age of instantaneous communication and action is reflex, not reflection, as Jacques Ellul has observed.[45] As our own thoughts become increasingly irrelevant, we compensate by retreating into fantasy and illusion.

Depersonalization occurs when a human being is treated as a nonperson. To handle a person as simply an inmate or as an abstract category, to define someone exclusively in terms of statistical information, or to act as if she were less than human is to depersonalize the other. But depersonalization runs in both directions. Under totalitarianism everyone is turned into a "cog in the machine." This in turn results in the obedience to authority syndrome or the bureaucratic mind. When faced with unlimited or arbitrary power, one must submit to it. Totalitarianism deprives individuals of their will. As Todorov observes, "Each and everyone is both guard and inmate at the same time."[46] Once again Todorov compares the dehumanizing aspects of modern bureaucracy and technology to totalitarian practices. Technology and bureaucracy mediate human relationships, permitting a vast increase in extensive, abstract relationships in the interest of efficiency at the expense of intensive, immediate relationships.[47] Abstract rules govern virtually all human relationships in modern organizations, including the university. Teaching, for example, is moving in the direction of a technical and contractual relationship between teacher and student in lieu of an informal, human relationship.

If the bureaucratic mind leads to submission to authority, it also results in its opposite—manipulation of others. In a universe of raw power, one submits to a power greater than one's own and manipulates that lesser strength. In such an environment moral judgment becomes superfluous, for everyone perceives that others invariably act out of self-interest.

The mass media reinforce and deepen the fragmentation and depersonalization that bureaucracy and technology unintentionally create. Television and related media are, in their overall impact, antinarrative. Although it can be argued that individual television programs have a narrative form (even here I argue that in the electronic media the visual images destroy the narrative structure of discourse), the entire spectrum of programs is random and incoherent. That is, there is no temporal and meaningful relationship among programs and commercials. One can go from the news of an earthquake to a commercial for hemorrhoids, to a talk show about men who are looking for a mother figure in the women they date, to a game show, to a program that recreates "true" police encounters with criminals. Therefore television in its total impact destroys the experience of event time. One is left with duration time, the continuous time of description. Television describes reality for us but leaves us with no understanding of it. The more television one watches, the more life appears absurd but interesting.

The main, if not exclusive, impact of the visual image is emotional.[48] Emotional experiences are principally aesthetical, and as such leave us oriented to the moment of pleasure or pain. By itself emotion does not allow us to transcend the immediate present. What is most distinctive about humans, Kierkegaard argues, is our imagination and anticipation of the future; without this, there is no sense of the past.[49] Television's visual images permit no future and thus no past. Television creates an eternal present. To live exclusively in the moment, to live from moment to moment, is to live a fragmented existence.

Television makes a fundamental appeal to our instincts. In short, television's images are pleasurable. Paul Goldberger maintains that "the rise in visual literacy has been accompanied by an almost desperate desire to be stimulated."[50] Our increased visual sophistication lowers our threshold for boredom; we require ever more spectacular experiences.

Television plays a large role in the representation of life as spectacle. According to Guy Debord, we now live in a world of visual representation, a mirror world in which the image is more important than and indeed defines reality. Moreover, all of life has been transformed into an image for immediate consumption. The spectacle is the "language" of the commodity; it is the visualization of the commodity for spiritual consumption.[51] The spectacle serves to reinforce the extreme individualism of consumerism. I possess as many selves as products I consume. Visual spectacle produces a feeling of unlimited power. Television and related media place me at the center of the universe. All images come to me, and I control them by switching channels. Moreover, television fills me up with information that I can share with the less informed. Because reality is on television, by watching television I gain a certain control—if only at the level of information—over reality. In both advertisements and programs, television titillates our desires and creates new needs. With the abolition of time, television destroys expectancy and delayed gratification; it creates a sense of immediate fulfillment.[52] The motto is, If I watch television these objects and images become mine. The power of television becomes the extent of my power.

Yet television destroys the reality of my solipsistic world by objectifying experience and providing me with secondhand emotions. Moreover, in their emotional impact, the visual images negate the distance between viewer and viewed. I become what I view. The visually oriented media indirectly

promote a vulgar pantheism.[53] In watching television, I fluctuate wildly between solipsism and pantheism.

Television makes discourse anonymous. It is information sent by no one
to anyone. It is impossible to trace the information back to a personal source,
for even newscasters often work from scripts written by others. The audience
is only a statistical audience of people with similar characteristics as determined by marketing techniques. Communication achieves its highest state of
impersonality in the media. The depersonalized information of the media
seems more objective than that provided by a person.

Walter Benjamin has called attention to the destruction of meaning that
occurs when a work of art is removed from its historical and cultural context
and is technologically reproduced exclusively as a visual image for consumption.[54] This objectification is essentially what television does on a much
larger scale.

Television appears to describe reality, particularly in news programs, doc-
umentaries, talk shows, and game shows. In effect, it is reconstructing reality
by taking reality out of its temporal and cultural context. Reality as we live
it still retains some meaning, no matter how slight; but television expunges
this meaning and recomposes reality as a sequence of image fragments. Television is antisurrealistic, as Ellul notes; it subtracts meaning from life.[55]

A former graduate student of mine talks about a special song that his girlfriend and he shared. When he heard the song, he thought about her and
their experiences together. Once he viewed the music video of that song, his
images were altered. Now when he heard the song, the images of the music
video appeared in his mind. His girlfriend and their experiences had van-
ished.

Poems, novels, and stories, by contrast, provide shared symbolic experiences to listeners and readers, which have to be filtered through the reader's
own meaningful experiences. The media objectify our experiences and thus
control them. Is this not a form of totalitarianism? And does this psychological totalitarianism not encourage schizophrenia?

A Dialectic of Paranoia and Schizophrenia

Paranoia and schizophrenia represent contradictory tendencies of a technological civilization—unity and fragmentation. The paranoid person creates a
unity of opposition to himself, just as the schizophrenic eventually becomes
hopelessly fragmented. The technological system creates a logical, statistical
unity through the computer, which coordinates the various technical subsystems. But it cannot create a symbolic unity, the only true cultural unity. In-

stead, the technological system leads to the fragmentation of culture and language. The paranoid schizophrenic embodies the opposing tendencies of unity and fragmentation at the psychological level; at the sociological level, the mass media institutionalize technological unity and cultural fragmentation. Paranoia and schizophrenia mirror the mass media.

Notes

1. David Bernstein, David Useda, and Larry Siever, "Paranoid Personality Disorder," in *The DSM-IV Personality Disorders*, ed. W. John Livesley (New York: Guilford, 1995), 49.

2. David Shapiro, *Neurotic Styles* (New York: Basic, 1965), 103.

3. Shapiro, *Neurotic Styles*, 54.

4. Shapiro, *Neurotic Styles*, 55–64.

5. Shapiro, *Neurotic Styles*, 64–68.

6. Shapiro, *Neurotic Styles*, 96.

7. Shapiro, *Neurotic Styles*, 74.

8. Shapiro, *Neurotic Styles*, 79–80.

9. Shapiro, *Neurotic Styles*, 81.

10. Shapiro, *Neurotic Styles*, 83.

11. Shapiro, *Neurotic Styles*, 95.

12. Shapiro, *Neurotic Styles*, 99.

13. Shapiro, *Neurotic Styles*, 93.

14. J. H. van den Berg, *A Different Existence* (Pittsburgh: Duquesne University Press, 1972), 110.

15. Joel Kovel, "Schizophrenic Being and Technocratic Society," in *Pathologies of the Modern Self*, ed. David Levin (New York: New York University Press, 1987), 332, 338.

16. R. D. Laing, *The Divided Self* (Middlesex, U.K.: Penguin, 1965), 43–49.

17. Louis Sass, *Madness and Modernism* (Cambridge: Harvard University Press, 1992), 14.

18. Sass, *Madness and Modernism*, 15.

19. Laing, *Divided Self*, 143.

20. Laing, *Divided Self*, 80.

21. Laing, *Divided Self*, 98.

22. Laing, *Divided Self*, chap. 5.

23. Laing, *Divided Self*, chap. 6.

24. Sass, *Madness and Modernism*, 11.

25. Laing, *Divided Self*, 108–10.

26. Laing, *Divided Self*, 117.

27. Laing, *Divided Self*, 138.

28. Laing, *Divided Self*, 158.

29. Laing, *Divided Self*, 161.

30. Kovel, "Schizophrenic Being and Technocratic Society," 337–38.

31. J. H. van den Berg, "On Hallucinating: Critical-Historical Overview and Guidelines for Further Study," in *Phenomenology and Psychiatry*, ed. A. J. J. De Koning and F. A. Jenner (New York: Academic, 1982), 105–8.

32. Sass, *Madness and Modernism*, 325–26, 353.

33. David Levin, "Psychopathology in the Epoch of Nihilism," in *Pathologies of the Modern Self*, 21–83.

34. Friedrich Juenger, *The Failure of Technology*, trans. Frederick Wilhelmsen (Chicago: Henry Regnery, 1956).

35. Max Weber, *Economy and Society*, vol. 2 (Berkeley: University of California Press, 1978), chap. 11.

36. John Aldridge, *The American Novel and the Way We Live Now* (New York: Oxford University Press, 1983), 9–16.

37. Thomas Pynchon, *The Crying of Lot 49* (New York: Bantam, 1967).

38. Karen Horney, *The Neurotic Personality of Our Time* (New York: Norton, 1937).

39. Edwin Lemert, "Paranoia and the Dynamics of Exclusion," *Sociometry*, March 1962, 2–20.

40. Jacques Ellul, *The Humiliation of the Word*, trans. Joyce Hanks (Grand Rapids, Mich.: Eerdmans, 1985), 148–54.

41. Owen Barfield, *Poetic Diction* (New York: McGraw-Hill, 1964).

42. Barfield, *Poetic Diction*, 209.

43. Tzvetan Todorov, *Facing the Extreme*, trans. Arthur Denner and Abigail Pollak (New York: Metropolitan, 1996).

44. Todorov, *Facing the Extreme*, chap. 8.

45. Jacques Ellul, *The Technological Society*, trans. John Wilkinson (New York: Vintage 1964), chap. 5.

46. Todorov, *Facing the Extreme*, 166.

47. *Facing the Extreme*, chap. 9.

48. E. H. Gombrich, "The Visual Image," *Scientific American*, September 1972, 82–96.

49. Søren Kierkegaard, *Concluding Unscientific Postscript*, trans. Howard Hong and Edna Hong (Princeton: Princeton University Press, 1992).

50. Paul Goldberger, "Design: The Risks of Razzle-Dazzle," *New York Times*, April 12, 1987, 1.

51. Guy Debord, *Society of the Spectacle* (Detroit: Black & Red, 1977).

52. Ellul, *Humiliation of the Word*, 208.

53. See Robert Pattison, *The Triumph of Vulgarity* (New York: Oxford University Press, 1987), for a discussion of vulgar pantheism.

54. Walter Benjamin, "The Work of Art in the Age of Mechanical Reproduction," in *Illuminations*, trans. Harry Zohn (New York: Schocken, 1969), 217–51.

55. Ellul, *Humiliation of the Word*, 140.

CHAPTER EIGHT

~

Shades of Loneliness

I began this book with the position taken by J. H. van den Berg—all disorders stem from the same sociological context and each disorder recapitulates the entire psychopathology. In this chapter we will see if my analysis gives credence to my starting assumptions.

The various neurotic styles and schizophrenia share many important characteristics. Even when one takes into account the manifest differences (e.g., the rationality of the obsessive-compulsive style and the irrationality of the impulsive style), the similarities greatly outweigh the differences. Except for those dominated by the neurotic need for affection (going toward others), the neurotic styles discussed in chapters 5–7 all involve a going against or a going away from others as the main way of handling neurotic anxiety. All neurotic styles involve a conflict between the actual self and an ideal self that is based on hatred of the former. The schizophrenic takes this to an extreme—a splitting of the inner self and false self. All disorders are characterized by chronic loneliness, a lack of spontaneity, a lack of affect, and some (for schizophrenics, nearly total) loss of reality.

The various neurotic styles and schizophrenia (psychosis) were previously related to contradictions of a technological civilization: the neurotic need for power and the neurotic need for affection to the contradiction between power and love; the obsessive-compulsive style and the impulsive style to the contradiction between rationality and irrationality; narcissism and depression to the contradiction between power and meaning; paranoia and schizophrenia to the contradiction between unity and fragmentation. Because these contradic-

141

tions flow from the same context—a technological civilization—they would seem to be interrelated. And indeed they are. The question of why some aspect of a technological society (e.g., meaninglessness as in depression, or the will to power as in narcissism) becomes more pronounced in any individual is due to her specific life circumstances and her personality.

From the preceding analysis, two commonly shared sets of characteristics emerge as most intimately related to the various technological contradictions: meaninglessness (nihilism, normlessness) and the will to power. Whether it takes the form of the impulsive's "lack of values" or the obsessive-compulsive's "loss of a sense of truth," all the disorders contain a commonly-recognized symptom—the experience of meaninglessness or normlessness. Depression is only the most full-blown example of what is involved in all the disorders. Those who suffer from the various disorders share as well a sense of powerlessness that is motivated by the will to power. The narcissist is the epitome of the individual driven by the will to power. I maintain that these important characteristics of all psychopathology—nihilism and the will to power—are psychological manifestations of the fundamental contradiction of a technological civilization.[1]

The contradiction between power and meaning, so that as power increases shared meaning decreases, is the ultimate source of the other cultural contradictions. My argument about a technological civilization suggests that as technical rationality (the power of technology) increases, so does irrationality (the power of instinct). The normlessness of a technological civilization gives free reign to both technical and instinctual power. Technology is simultaneously the paramount organizing and disorganizing force in modern societies; it provides a unity in the technological system but leaves in its wake cultural fragmentation. Only a symbolic and moral unity allows humans to experience life as a unified narrative. The relationship between the contradiction of power and meaning and that between power and love is perhaps the most obvious. Love is at once an action and an idea (symbol or concept). In a state of meaninglessness, love begins to mimic power (love as manipulation, overprotection). Therefore, the contradiction between power and meaning is the source of the other contradictions. This, I suggest, explains why accounts of the symptoms of all these disorders include meaninglessness and the will to power as salient characteristics.

How is the technological personality related to these psychological disorders? The technological personality allows one to internalize some of the visual and auditory stimuli of a technological society, thereby creating a kind of stimulus shield; but it is no help with the problem of perpetual loneliness. Indeed it reinforces and deepens loneliness because the technological personality militates against establishing sincere relationships. One is left with role-playing and shallow emotions.

The technological personality entails a split between the subjective and objective (secondhand emotions and experiences) and the inner (the lonely, uncertain self) and the outer (the extraverted personality). Moreover, psychological life since the late eighteenth century has witnessed the development of multiple selves. Given the blurring of the distinction between the normal and the neurotic, on the one hand, and between the neurotic and the psychotic, on the other hand, one is left with the sad and shocking thought that *schizophrenia takes the technological personality to its logical conclusion.*

Today we are all lonely and suffer from the scourge of multiple selves, but not to the same extent. Some are blessed with families, friends, neighborhoods, and communities that mitigate to some extent the culturally and psychologically disorganizing power of a technological civilization. Family and friends have tacitly resisted the nihilism of a technological society and have chosen to lead their lives according to some moral custom. They have become an oasis in the desert of normlessness. Moral custom is, however, just that—custom. As such it is fighting a losing battle against the prevailing standards of the mass media.[2] Time is running out. We must redefine a common morality for our time—the time of technological domination.

In *Imperfect Garden*, Tzvetan Todorov argues in favor of a universal humanistic morality. He holds that such a morality is commensurate with the identity of the human race. Its basic tenets—"autonomy of the *I*, finality of the *you*, universality of the *they*"—are self-evident.[3] In an earlier study of Nazi and Russian concentration camps, Todorov defined "caring" as the most important universal "ordinary virtue." But he was unwilling to accept a definition of caring that is based on altruism, especially suffering. In his view, caring should be mutually beneficial and thus a source of happiness. Yet he acknowledges that there are times when heroic or saintly virtues are called for. By his own admission, however, the latter are invariably based on religious and/or political beliefs.

Todorov observes that modern technological societies have totalitarian tendencies, which reached their apogee in concentration camps. In his view, totalitarianism cannot be opposed solely by the practice of ordinary virtues like caring. Instead, we must employ political and legal means. But politics, like religion, poses dangers because it often leads believers to subordinate people to abstract causes. Todorov acknowledges, however, that a few have been able to combine religious or political belief and a "morality of sympathy" (as opposed to a "morality of principle"), such as the rescuers who helped Jews escape the Nazis.[4]

What Todorov fails to understand is that love is the most radical act of all when it contains an element of suffering, the suffering with others, the co-feeling of compassion.[5] At this moment love becomes heroic or saintly. Love, moreover, is intimately related to freedom. Love is the meaning of and the limitation on freedom. At the same time, love presupposes freedom; only free people can fully love others.[6] Modern technological societies transform power into a value and thus turn freedom and love into luxuries. To oppose the fragmenting and depersonalizing tendencies of a technological society, one must freely practice the ordinary virtue of caring (love). Will the "identity of the human race" be able to motivate us to rescue others from loneliness?

Notes

1. In David Levin, "Psychopathology in the Epoch of Nihilism," in *Pathologies of the Modern Self*, ed. David Levin (New York: New York University Press, 1987), 22–83, there is a recognition that the will to power drives narcissism, depression, and schizophrenia. Moreover, he relates the will to power to nihilism. But the analysis of the larger sociological context—technocratic and capitalistic—is left undeveloped.

2. Richard Stivers, *The Culture of Cynicism* (Cambridge: Blackwell, 1994).

3. Tzvetan Todorov, *Imperfect Garden*, trans. Carol Cosman (Princeton: Princeton University Press, 2002), 40.

4. Tzvetan Todorov, *Facing the Extreme: Moral Life in Concentration Camps* (New York: Metropolitan, 1996), 220–28.

5. Milan Kundera, *The Unbearable Lightness of Being*, trans. Michael Heim (New York: Harper & Row, 1984), 20–21.

6. Jacques Ellul, *The Ethics of Freedom*, trans. Geoffrey Bromiley (Grand Rapids, Mich.: Eerdmans, 1976), 206–10.

Index

advertising, 102, 110–12, 121. *See also* television

aesthetical: as dimension of culture, 9; as existence-sphere, 9

Aldridge, John, 134, 135

Alger, Horatio, 82

Andren, Gunnar, 111

anomie, 56–61, 65, 66, 70, 85. *See also* pluralism

anxiety, 62, 63, 65, 66

Arendt, Hanna, 98

Arney, William, 3

attention deficit disorder, 3, 48–49

authenticity, 11–12, 77

Balzac, Honoré, 114

Barfield, Owen, 23

Barth, John, 103

Baudrillard, Jean, 114

Baumgartner, M. P., 2, 18

Benjamin, Walter, 140

Bergen, Bernard, 3

Bon Marché (department store), 113, 115

Boorstin, Daniel, 20, 57

boredom. *See* meaninglessness

Brod, Craig, 48, 49

Brooks, David, 37

Brun, Jean, 116

Campbell, Colin, 115

Canetti, Elias, 84

Carnegie, Dale, 112

Carpenter, Edmund, 19

character, 9, 12, 13, 16

character types: inner-directed, 13–14; other-directed, 13–14, 16, 28, 97; tradition-directed, 13

Cohen, Sheldon, 42

"cold child." *See* television

computer, 21, 25, 35, 37, 44, 45, 49, 69, 134. *See also* mass media

Conrad, Peter, 3

consumption, 14, 22, 35–36, 39, 108, 112–15, 120–21, 123; as meaning of life, 36, 115–16, 139; related to identity, 114, 139

Crosby, Alfred, 23

culture: of fear, 1, 123; of forgetting, 24; spurious, 3, 6

Darwin, Charles, 83
Debord, Guy, 139
Delillo, Don, 41, 114, 134
depersonalization, 130, 137, 138, 140, 146. *See also* fragmentation
depression, 41, 103, 108–9, 118, 123
deviance, 3
Diamond, Stanley, 5, 56
Diderot, Denis, 11
Dostoevsky, Fyodor, 85
Douglas, Ann, 78–79, 86
Dreiser, Theodore, 82
Dumont, Louis, 85
Durkheim, Emile, 56

Eichmann, Adolf, 98
Elias, Norbert, 12
Ellul, Jacques, 22, 25, 37, 38, 39, 50, 66–68, 70, 101, 116, 119, 120, 138, 140
equality: and love, 85; norm of, 60–61, 85; and power, 85
ethical: as dimension of culture, 9; as existence-sphere, 9

false meaning, 120–22. *See also* consumption
fragmentation: cultural, 6, 124, 137, 138, 141, 143, 144, 146; psychological, 100, 131–33, 137, 140, 146. *See also* depersonalization; schizophrenia
Franklin, Benjamin, 37, 81
Frazer, Jill, 45
Freud, Sigmund, 2, 47, 59, 61

Gehlen, Arnold, 18, 21
Gerbner, George, 40
Glassner, Barry, 1
Goldberger, Paul, 139
Gottlieb, Beatrice, 75–77
Green, Arnold, 88–89
Greene, Theodore, 84

Greene, Tom, 26
Gross, Larry, 40
Grumet, Gerald, 97

Harris, Neil, 115
Healy, Jane, 48, 49
Hendin, Herbert, 86, 102
Hendin, Josephine, 103
Herberg, Will, 17
Herrick, Robert, 82
Hochschild, Arlie, 26, 36
Hofstadter, Richard, 83
hopelessness, 109, 118, 122. *See also* meaninglessness
Horney, Karen, 5, 55, 61–66, 70, 84, 86, 95, 108, 135
Horwitz, Allan, 2, 3, 6
Huizinga, J. H., 25, 88
hyperactivity, 48–49
hyperreflexivity, 23, 132

impulsive style, 96–97, 100, 102, 143
"intimate terrorism," 87

James, Henry, 114
James, William, 83
Juenger, Friedrich, 109

Kahler, Erich, 23
Kierkegaard, Søren, 9–10, 14–16, 122, 131, 139
Kovel, Joel, 5, 108, 130, 133
Kraut, Robert, 41
Kundera, Milan, 38

Laing, R. D., 130–32
Larkin, Ralph, 118
Leiss, William, 111
Lemert, Edwin, 135
Levin, David, 5, 107
Levine, Robert, 34
Lewis, Sinclair, 114
Linder, Steffan, 35

literature: anarchic, 103; holistic, 103
London, Jack, 82
loneliness, 1, 2, 4, 6, 7, 24, 26, 27, 41, 50, 55, 60, 63, 144, 145
love: as dependency, 8, 9, 90; as part of discipline, 77; as personality absorption, 88–89; and power, 86–90; romantic, 76; sentimental, 78–80, 86, 87
Lowenthal, Leo, 112
Lundmark, Vicki, 41

Mander, Jerry, 19, 48
Marx, Karl, 43, 97
mass media, 18–19, 20, 21, 48–49, 101, 102, 138, 141. See also television
McLuhan, Marshall, 70
meaninglessness, 24, 95, 103, 108, 109, 118–20, 122, 123, 133, 144. See also hopelessness; powerlessness
mental disease, 2–3, 6
mental disorder, 2–3, 6, 7, 143
mental illness, 2–3. See also mental disease; mental disorder
Milgran, Stanley, 98–99
Miller, Michael, 87, 113, 115
Mills, C. Wright, 98
multiple selves, 4, 58, 65. See also schizophrenia

narcissism, 103, 107–8, 109, 116, 123
neurotic need: for affection, 62–63, 89–90; for power, 63, 89–90, 108
neurotic style, 93
Niebuhr, H. Richard, 81
Nietzsche, Friedrich, 10, 12, 85
nihilism. See meaninglessness
Norris, Frank, 82
North, Oliver, 98

obedience to authority, 97–99, 100
obsessive-compulsive disorder, 93–96, 97, 102, 143, 144

paranoia, 124, 127–30, 133–35, 140, 141, 143
Peale, Norman Vincent, 112
personality, 9, 13, 16; inner, 26–27, 28, 50, 145; objective, 19–24, 28, 145; outer, 26–27, 28, 50, 145; subjective, 24–26, 28, 145; technological, 6, 19–28, 46–50, 55, 144, 145
Phillips, David, 82
pluralism, 57–58, 65
Polakow, Valerie, 87
Postman, Neil, 87, 110
powerlessness, 24, 25, 108, 109, 116, 117
psychopathology, 2, 6, 56. See also mental illness
psychosis. See schizophrenia
public opinion, 14–16, 18, 20, 101
puerilism, 25–26, 88
Pynchon, Thomas, 103, 121, 134, 135

Riesman, David, 13, 14, 61, 112, 121
Rousseau, Jean-Jacques, 11

Saper, Edward, 3
Sass, Louis, 4, 5, 131, 132
Schivelbusch, Wolfgang, 46–48
schizophrenia, 4, 5, 124, 127, 130–33, 135, 140, 141, 143, 145
Schumpeter, Joseph, 84, 117
Seabrook, Jeremy, 119
secondhand emotions, 21
self: false, 131–32, 143; idealized, 64, 108; inner, 131–33, 143; moral, 10; real, 64
sentimentality. See love
sentiment of being, 11–12
Shapiro, David, 93–97, 127, 130
Shorter, Edward, 76
Simmel, Georg, 23, 47
sincerity, 11
Smith, Adam, 58
sociosis, 7, 55

solipsism, 133. *See also* schizophrenia
Sorokin, Pitirim, 58
Spencer, Herbert, 83
stimulus shield, 46–49, 50, 55
stress: and communication, 38–41; and
 crowding and noise, 41–42; and
 tempo of society, 34–38; and workplace, 42–46
success: as efficiency, 84; material,
 82–84; true, 82–83
Summer, William Graham, 83

Tawney, Richard, 80
technological fatalism, 116–17
technological utopianism, 26, 110
technology: and consciousness, 23; contradictions of, 6–7, 69–72, 102–3,
 123–24, 143; and memory, 37, 49; as
 milieu, 67, 68–69; and power, 24, 71,
 72, 109; as sacred, 116; as system, 67,
 69, 134, 144
television, 21, 27, 28, 35, 39–41, 48–49,
 138–40. *See also* mass media
Terkel, Studs, 118, 119
Tocqueville, Alexis de, 12, 18, 80

Todorov, Tzvetan, 85, 137–38,
 145–46
Trilling, Lionel, 11, 12
Trow, George, 27
Turner, Victor, 5

Ulrich, 23
unconscious, 59

Van den Berg, J. H., 2, 4, 5, 7, 28,
 55–61, 66, 70, 75, 85, 89, 97, 130,
 131, 133, 143
Van Dyke, John, 83
Vonnegut, Kurt, 103

Wakefield, Jerome, 2, 3
Weber, Max, 97, 134
Weinstein, Neil, 42
Whyte, William, 27
Wilde, Oscar, 12
will to power, 116, 144
Wolfenstein, Martha, 12

Zelizer, Viviana, 79
Zuboff, Shoshana, 99

~

About the Author

Richard Stivers is professor of sociology at Illinois State University. He is author of *A Hair of the Dog: Irish Drinking and American Stereotype; Evil in Modern Myth and Ritual; The Culture of Cynicism: American Morality in Decline;* and *Technology as Magic: The Triumph of the Irrational.*